'*Pick Your Brains* children's travel guides for 8-12-year-olds stimulate children's in⟨…⟩ ⟨…⟩ut being heavy handed … Ple⟨…⟩ ⟨…⟩th the kind of irreverence kids lo⟨…⟩

'Any family heading ⟨…⟩ ⟨…⟩ a copy of the excellent *Pick You⟨…⟩* ⟨…⟩ children. Excellently designed, ⟨…⟩ ⟨…⟩ the benefit of a twelve-year-old "guest editor" to keep the authors clued in to the facts and sights that will intrigue a young reader and drive adults mad with their questions.' Dermot Bolger, **Dublin Evening Herald**

'Let your child impress poolside companions and dinner guests on your costa holiday by spouting amusing anecdotes and informative tidbits about Spanish life and society, all harvested from this jolly piece of literature. Not a guidebook in the traditional sense, the series helps kids explore the culture and history of the country they are visiting with entertaining stories behind local customs, festivals and food.' *[Pick Your Brains About Spain]*, Gemma Bowes, **Observer**

'A new travel guide for kids will keep little minds occupied for hours … *Pick Your Brains*, is a fun fact-filled series … the perfect antidote to plane/train/automobile rage.' **Irish Independent**

'some of this is fascinating and delivered in the sort of language many children will like.' *[Pick Your Brains About Italy]*, Books of the Week, **Sunday Times**

'*Pick Your Brains About England*, an alternative tourist guide for eight to twelve-year-olds, is one of four books that explain the history of European countries in a light but informative way.' **Irish Times**

'A handy guide to great places to visit… Some of the places sound fab and you would never have heard about without a guidebook… it's all really clear and a cracking read.' ★★★★ review of the series, **Newsround** *website, BBC 1*

'*Pick Your Brains About England* will help bookworms swot up on their knowledge of England. There are cartoons and plenty of info on attractions, food and sport.' **Daily Express**

'These books tell you all about France, Spain, England and Italy... Did you know that the Italians have a festival of chocolate or that the Spanish throw tomatoes at each other? And as for the English, did you know someone once tried to eat every animal known to man?' *Blue Peter* website, BBC 1

'A fun new children's travel book *Pick Your Brains about England* has the answers ... and apart from fascinating facts, tells you the best places to visit.' *The People*

'Curious kids? If you need quick answers to holiday questions from inquisitive eight to twelve-year-olds, take a look at *Pick Your Brains About* ... packed with puzzles, facts and figures.' *Sainsbury's Magazine*

'This new book series for kids lifts the lid on various holiday destinations, including Italy, France, England and this one, Spain. It's an involving introduction to España with sections of various sights, festivals, history, phrases and customs ... it's very readable. Olé!' *Funday Times, Sunday Times*

'Canny publishers have come up with fun and easily accessible guidebooks aimed exclusively at children – not a bad idea when you consider children often choose the family holiday ... a witty series.' Chloë Bryan-Brown, *The Times* (Travel)

'*Pick Your Brains* is a fantastically fun travel series ... It introduces the cultures and customs of four European countries through their food, history, landmarks, famous figures and recommends the very best places to visit.' *Quiz Kids*

'For more fun facts about Spain, pick up the children's travel guide series *Pick Your Brains About...*' *easyJet Magazine*

The Pick Your Brains series

England by Leo Hollis • *France* by Marian Pashley • *Greece* by Caroline Sanderson • *Italy* by Jez Mathews • *Scotland* by Mandy Kirkby • *Spain* by Mandy Kirkby • *USA* by Jane Egginton

PICK YOUR BRAINS
about
IRELAND

Mary O'Neill

Illustrations by
Caspar Williams & Craig Dixon

CADOGAN

Acknowledgements

The author and the publisher would like to thank 'guest editors'
Síofra Sloyan Ní Thuathaláin (aged 10) and Muireann McCann (aged 12).

Warmest thanks to family and friends in Ireland, and to Dermot.

Published by Cadogan Guides 2005
Copyright © Mary O'Neill 2005

Illustrations by Caspar Williams and Craig Dixon
Illustrations and map copyright © Cadogan Guides 2005
Map by ⓣⓦ

Cadogan Guides
Network House, 1 Ariel Way, London W12 7SL
info@cadoganguides.co.uk
www.cadoganguides.com

The Globe Pequot Press
246 Goose Lane, PO Box 480, Guilford,
Connecticut 06437–0480

Design and typesetting by Mathew Lyons
Printed in Italy by Legoprint

A catalogue record for this book is available
from the British Library
ISBN 1-86011-221-8

Contents

Not to scale!

Vital Facts
and Figures

Size and location: The island of Ireland has an area of 84,433 square kilometres (32,595 square miles). It is about 450km (300 miles) long from north to south, and about 300km (190 miles) wide from west to east. It is the most northwesterly country in the European Union and the 20th-largest island in the world.

To the west lies the Atlantic Ocean and, as people in western Ireland say, 'next stop, America'. The Irish Sea, to the east, and the North Channel, to the north and northeast, separate Ireland from its nearest neighbour, Britain. Rathlin Island, in Northern Ireland, is just 19km from the Mull of Kintyre in Scotland. The nearest continental European country is France, across the Celtic Sea.

The island of Ireland is made up of the Republic of Ireland and Northern Ireland. Like Scotland, Wales and England, Northern Ireland is governed as part of the United Kingdom. The other four-fifths of the island form a country with a separate government, a parliament called the Oireachtas, a prime minister called the Taoiseach and a president as the head of state. In the UK this country is often referred to as 'Éire' or 'Southern Ireland', to differentiate it from Northern Ireland. In the Republic, however, the word 'Éire' (which means 'Ireland') is used on passports, official papers and stamps. People refer to their home country as 'Ireland' and never actually say 'Éire'. Sometimes you will see 'ROI', which is short for the 'Republic of Ireland'.

Funnily enough, just when you think you've got the hang of things, you find out that the most northerly tip of Ireland is actually in 'the South'. It's enough to make a cat laugh!

Next stop America!

Provinces and counties:
The island as a whole is divided into four ancient provinces or regions: Leinster, Munster, Connacht and Ulster. The 26 counties of the Republic are:

☞ **Leinster** (to the east)
Carlow, Dublin, Kildare, Kilkenny, Laois, Longford, Louth, Meath, Offaly, Westmeath, Wexford, Wicklow

☞ **Munster** (to the south)
Clare, Cork, Kerry, Limerick, Tipperary, Waterford

☞ **Connacht** (to the west)
Galway, Leitrim, Mayo, Roscommon, Sligo

☞ **Ulster** (to the north)
The three Ulster counties in the Republic are:
Cavan, Donegal, Monaghan

The province of Ulster contains the border between the Republic and Northern Ireland. This border is about 450km (280 miles) long and has been open since 1994. Before that, security checkpoints and customs points were in operation.

The six counties in Northern Ireland are:
Antrim, Armagh, Derry (or Londonderry), Down,
Fermanagh, Tyrone.

Try FAT DAD or FAT LAD as a memory trick for these.

Capital cities: The capital of the Republic of Ireland is Dublin, on the east coast. The population of the city and county of Dublin stands at more than 1,100,000. About a third of the country's total population lives in the Greater Dublin area.

Belfast, on the northeast coast, is the capital city of Northern Ireland and is home to more than 645,000 people. More than 16 per cent of the total population of Northern Ireland live in Belfast.

Languages: The Republic has two official languages, Irish (or Gaelic) and English. English is spoken everywhere. Some people living in Gaeltacht areas speak Irish as their first language. These Irish-speaking areas are in Cork, Donegal, Galway, Kerry, Mayo, Meath and Waterford. In 2002 more

---

═ *Other major cities* ═

In the Republic:

☞ **Cork** (120,000 people), on the south coast

☞ **Galway** (65,000), on the west coast

☞ **Limerick** (54,000), a little further south of Galway

☞ **Waterford** (44,500), to the southeast

In Northern Ireland:

☞ **Derry City** (105,000), Northern Ireland's second city

☞ **Armagh** (54,000), an important historic and religious centre

---

than 42 per cent of the Republic's population said that they could speak some Irish. But most of those who actually use it do so at school.

In Northern Ireland English is the official language. The local dialect of the northeastern part of the province is called Ulster Scots. The Irish language is also taught and spoken in Northern Ireland.

Climate: The climate is fairly mild and temperatures range from about 4–7°C in January and February to 14–17°C in July and August. On average, it rains on about 150 days in the year in the east and southeast, and up to 225 days a year in parts of the west.

Terrain: Ireland may have become an island as recently as 6500 BC, after the Great Ice Age. It's a bit like a saucer, with mountains around the coasts and a low, central midlands area. The mountains are smooth rather than jagged, and not as high as continental mountain ranges. The highest peak on the whole island, at 1,039 metres (3,409 feet), is Carrauntoohil in County Kerry.

At a length of 257km (160 miles), the Shannon is the longest river in Ireland, England, Scotland and Wales.

The largest lake, on both islands, is Lough Neagh. Five of Northern Ireland's six counties have shores on this large inland sea, which covers 383 square kilometres (148 square miles). The story is that when the giant Finn McCool ripped up a lump of earth and flung it into the Irish Sea, the hole left behind became Lough Neagh and that same lump of earth became the Isle of Man... but that's just a legend!

Coastline: The total length of the Irish coastline is 7,800km (4,800 miles). To the west and the north the Atlantic coastline is rugged, with lots of rocky headlands, inlets and islands. The northeastern part of the island has volcanic rock formations, while the eastern and southern coasts have stretches of sandy beaches.

Population: The population of the island as a whole is currently about 5.6 million, with 3.9 million living in the Republic and 1.7 million in Northern Ireland.

Favourite drink: Irish people drink more tea per person than any other nation in the world – that's 3.6 kg of the stuff per person per year.

Time zone: Ireland is on Greenwich Mean Time (GMT).

Internet and mobiles: The Republic's domain name is .ie. In 2002 90 per cent of people aged between 15 and 25 owned mobile phones. Irish mobile users had sent 1.5 billion text messages by 2001.

Currency: The euro is used in the Republic of Ireland and the pound sterling is used in Northern Ireland.

In 2002 the euro replaced the Irish pound or punt. The punt, too, was quite different from sterling, both in appearance and value. Famous Irish figures, such as Queen Maeve of Connacht, James Joyce, W.B. Yeats and Jonathan Swift were featured on colourful bank notes, and several of the coins had Celtic designs. Before the punt came in, in 1979, the Irish and British currencies were linked. Throughout all the changes the harp has remained on the reverse of all coins in the Republic of Ireland.

Though the currency used in Northern Ireland is the same as that used in England, Scotland and Wales, you'll also find Northern Irish banknotes in circulation.

Main industries and exports: One in three of all the PCs sold in Europe is manufactured in the Republic of Ireland. It is the largest exporter of software in the world and a third of Irish exports are information technology products.

Tourism is also a major industry, with more than six million people visiting the country every year. The most popular destinations are Dublin, the southwest and the

west of Ireland.

Agriculture now accounts for only about 7 per cent of the Republic's exports. The main activities are cattle-rearing and dairy farming. In 2002 there were 6,992,000 cattle in the Republic. That means that cattle outnumbered people by almost two to one!

Northern Ireland is Europe's second largest producer of linen, and exports large amounts to the US and the rest of Europe. The linen industry is one of Ulster's oldest industries, along with shipbuilding.

Ferries and planes: Dublin and Belfast are the island's main ports. Other ferry ports are Dun Laoghaire, Rosslare and Cork. Ferries leave Larne in Northern Ireland for Stranraer in Scotland.

The main international airports are at Dublin, Cork, Belfast and Shannon. At Shannon, near Limerick, you can sort out US immigration formalities while still in Ireland. It saves time queuing once you get to America! Shannon also had the world's first ever duty-free shop.

Trains: The railway system in Ireland is run by two different companies, north and south of the border. Iarnród Éireann (Irish Railways) operates the network in the Republic. Northern Ireland Rail runs the railways north of the border.

If you look at a map of Ireland showing just the rail connections, you'll see that a very large part of the northwest region of the Republic and the centre of Northern Ireland is completely blank. You cannot get on a train in Dublin or Cork and get off anywhere 'up north' in County Donegal. Dundalk on the east coast is the only town close to the border with Northern Ireland that you can get to by train from anywhere else in the Republic. Things were tough for the railways in the 1950s and Donegal's last lines closed in 1959. Almost 80 per cent of Northern Ireland's inland connections were also closed down and the main railway line now runs along the northeastern coastline only.

Frequent fast trains run between Dublin and Belfast, and from Belfast to the city of Derry. Many people living near local airports such as Sligo, Donegal and Derry prefer flying.

The DART and the LUAS: Dublin has a commuter rail link called the DART (short for Dublin Area Rapid Transit). It runs along the coast between Howth, to the north of the city, and Bray in County Wicklow.

The LUAS light rail transit system is a new tram system operating in the capital. Pronounced like 'lewis' (it means 'speed' in Irish), the LUAS lines connect the city centre with the suburbs. It was developed to ease Dublin's chronic traffic problems. The LUAS opened to the public in June 2004, with free rides for the first three days. Older Dubliners smile as the ultra-modern LUAS runs along some very old tram lines, which were closed down 45 years ago.

Buses: In the South, Bus Éireann is Ireland's answer to the Greyhound buses of the US. In fact, the company logo features a dashing Irish setter. Ulsterbus operates around 1,100 buses to all corners of Northern Ireland. Buses from both companies travel north and south of the border. Dublin and Belfast also have their own citywide bus services. Some Dubliners call them 'banana buses' (because they travel in bunches, geddit?)

Irish History in a Nutshell

Prehistoric and Celtic Ireland

Ireland has been inhabited for about 7,000 years. The first
visitors were nomads and hunters who arrived between 8000
and 4000 BC possibly from Scotland. Some of the earliest
signs of human activity in Ireland are to be found near
Coleraine in Northern Ireland.

The hunting tribes were followed from about 3000 BC
onwards by settlers who kept animals and farmed the land.
The countryside is dotted with dolmens, standing stones and
burial mounds as reminders of this prehistoric age. Many of
the sites overlook the Irish Sea or the Atlantic Ocean.

There were no towns, just individual dwellings. The
remains of up to 40,000 ancient ring forts can be found
around the country. As the name suggests, these stone forts
are circular in shape. They are often located on spectacular
hilltops and even on cliff edges. These locations probably
had a religious significance, but they were also good places
for spotting trouble coming from a distance – and you could
always count on trouble! Inside the ring fort, people kept
their animals and property safe from raiders.

Other people lived in lake dwellings or crannógs. These were makeshift wooden huts protected by high timber fences, built in marshy areas and even on artificial islands.

Around 600 BC a people very skilled in handling metals like iron and gold began to arrive in Ireland from central Europe. They were the Celts. They brought with them a language that eventually became Irish. They made weapons, but also beautiful jewellery and objects decorated with ornate spiral patterns. They also brought with them a rich culture of poetry, storytelling and music.

Poets and storytellers were hugely important in Celtic society, second only to

19

the kings. The poets depended on their kings, so naturally they praised them. On the other hand, a chieftain who annoyed a poet could find himself ridiculed in a poem. The poem would then be recited the length and breadth of the kingdom. If word went round that the chieftain was a poor host, his reputation would be ruined. The poets also kept track of royal family trees and helped to decide who would be next to rule a kingdom. The oldest in the family didn't automatically get to boss the others around! Poets were, in a word, powerful.

The Celts were pretty fierce warriors, but they were also farmers who raised cattle. Cattle were a sign of a person's wealth and importance. The more powerful chieftains made lesser families pay them tax in the form of cattle. There was a lot of fighting between the different petty kingdoms in Ireland. (Now there's a surprise.) There was no single, all-powerful ruler, called a High King, for a very long time.

From slave to bishop to big, big parades

The Romans never colonized Ireland. However, their settlements in Wales and England were constantly raided by Irish pirates in search of loot and slaves. Magonus Succatus Patricius, a boy of about 15, ended up on a slave ship and spent six years herding animals in either County Antrim or, possibly, County Mayo. The details are vague, but it was definitely grim! Though he managed to escape and return home, he experienced visions of the Irish calling him to

---

You can see early Christian Ireland:

☞ at Clonmacnoise, County Offaly;

☞ at the Rock of Cashel, County Tipperary;

☞ in the Celtic high crosses at Monasterboice, Moone, Carndonagh, Ardboe.

---

return, which he did some time in the 5th century. He wasn't the first Christian missionary to come to Ireland and, during this period, many monasteries were founded throughout the island. He established a community in Downpatrick, County Down, where he is thought to be buried. He remains the saint most closely associated with Ireland and his feast day, 17 March, is celebrated by Irish and non-Irish alike all around the world, but especially in the United States. You've guessed it – he was St Patrick!

Saints, scholars... and loads of treasure

The early Irish monks kept records of both historical events and myths. They also created beautifully illustrated books telling the stories of Christianity. Sometimes you can find doodles on the sides of the pages! These books are fabulous in their design and colours, but can you imagine how long it must have taken to copy every single detail down? They mixed Celtic patterns and Christianity, and

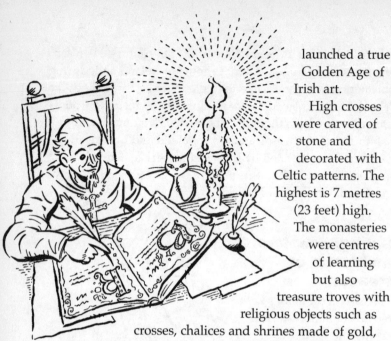

launched a true Golden Age of Irish art.

High crosses were carved of stone and decorated with Celtic patterns. The highest is 7 metres (23 feet) high. The monasteries were centres of learning but also treasure troves with religious objects such as crosses, chalices and shrines made of gold, jewels and precious stones. While much of the Roman empire in Europe had fallen to the barbarians, Irish monks travelled all over the continent, establishing monasteries as far afield as Switzerland, Italy and Germany. Soon, however, people would be travelling in the other direction. Some came almost by invitation, others were less welcome.

Viking newcomers

From the 9th century onwards, Viking raiding parties in longships arrived from the far north. The Irish knew them as 'dark foreigners' (from Denmark) and 'fair foreigners' (from Norway). The raiders headed straight for the monasteries, where they knew they would find food, livestock and above all treasure. Many tall, chimney-shaped towers with conical roofs, known as round towers, date from this period. Although they were actually bell-towers, they had no easy access from the outside (the tiny doorways are located 10 feet from the ground), and so they were the monks' best bet for safety. The Vikings weren't the only ones giving them a headache. The monasteries were frequently raided by the Irish as well!

Gradually the Vikings began to settle and trade in coastal areas, establishing the very first towns in Ireland. Their settlements were located in sheltered inlets – reminders of the fjords back home. There was, however, constant warfare

between the native Irish and the Vikings. The King of Munster, Brian Ború, emerged as the strongest Irish leader. The decisive battle between his forces and the Vikings of Dublin took place in 1014 at Clontarf, now a suburb of Dublin. The Vikings and their allies from Norway and Iceland were massively defeated, and the event is even mentioned in one of their sagas. Brian was killed as victory was announced, but he has the great honour of having a pub named after him in Dublin.

Norman invaders

In 1166, exactly 100 years after the Battle of Hastings, the first Norman armies arrived in Waterford and, within a month, they had taken Dublin. They had come to 'assist' an Irish king to regain control of his kingdom. They were followed by King Henry II, who was proclaimed Lord of Ireland. Henry established a network of barons and nobles, to whom he gave lands throughout the country in return for their loyalty. Some Irish chieftains also swore allegiance to Henry. Others, to the north and the west, never accepted the newcomers.

The Norman barons began building castles and forts in mainly fertile lands, while the mountainous territories remained in the hands of the native Irish. Most of the main inland towns in Ireland were built by Norman landowners. By 1230 Dublin Castle had been built by King John. Dublin

and nearby parts of Leinster beca.
Everywhere else was simply 'beyon.
after they first arrived, the Normans h.
three-quarters of Ireland. They brought a
of government, new laws (very different fro.
laws) and new coins.

But total control wasn't easy. Many Normans ¡

The Cattle Raid of Cooley

This is a legend from the time of the Celts in Ireland. Maeve, Queen of Connacht, and her husband Ailill were forever competing to see who had the most possessions. Maeve was disgusted to find that she had nothing to compare with Ailill's prize white bull. There was only one other bull in Ireland to equal it, the brown bull of Cooley in Ulster, a kingdom ruled by Conor MacNessa. Maeve asked to borrow the bull and, when her request was refused, she decided to take it anyway.

It so happened that the knights of Ulster were under a spell and incapable of defending the kingdom against the Connacht invaders. Only a 17-year-old boy named Cúchulainn stood between Maeve's army and the bull of Cooley. He challenged Maeve to send her soldiers, one by one, to fight him. This she did, but each one was defeated. Ferdia, one of the soldiers Cúchulainn had to fight to the death, had been his close friend. Ferdia really had to insult Cúchulainn in order to get him to fight. No prizes for guessing who won, although they had to battle it out for three days.

Cúchulainn was the greatest mythical warrior in Ireland, but Ferdia's name lives on in Ardee. The town in County Louth gets its name from the place in the river where Ferdia fell, mortally wounded. In Dublin, this story is depicted in a huge wall mosaic in Nassau Street.

marrying and
opting their clothing,
language and customs.
Major events such as
the Black Death,
England's wars
against France and
non-stop power struggles
made it difficult for the
king in England to keep
control over the goings on
in Ireland. The
influence of the Pale
began to dwindle. This
left the old and the new
Irish free to do more or less as
they liked. When the Tudors gained the throne of England,
however, they meant business both at home and in Ireland.

An unruly colony

Before the time of Henry VIII, the English kings relied on the
loyalty of leading Irish families to run the country for them.
Henry, however, was a more hands-on king. Immediately,
political or religious troubles in England and continental
Europe began to affect Ireland. Henry's new Protestant
religion did not take hold there and the people remained
Catholic. Europe's wars of religion had arrived and would
stay for many, many years to come.

Elizabeth I, Henry's daughter, was worried that her
enemy, the Catholic King Philip II of Spain, would use
Ireland as a base from which to attack England. It was
during her reign that the English colonization of much of
Ireland really began. Families were encouraged to leave
England and settle in large areas of the country. The plan

was to ensure loyalty to the crown in Ireland, but it also caused a lot of anger. After a failed attempt at rebellion against Elizabeth (involving Spanish support, as she feared), many of the most important Irish nobles left their ancestral lands in Ulster for continental Europe, never to return.

New settlers were brought into Ulster from Scotland and England to develop lands confiscated from the local Irish. As well as their Protestant faith and their English language, they brought with them a very different way of life. They grew crops, rather than raising cattle, and established industries in weaving and woolmaking. They built towns. But resentment among the native population at the loss of their lands continued to seethe. It was a violent age.

When Oliver Cromwell arrived in 1649, his task was to regain control of a troublesome colony. His first actions on arrival were to slaughter the entire populations of two towns, Wexford and Drogheda, which had tried to resist. Hearing news of the massacres, other towns quickly surrendered. More land was confiscated. By the time Charles II had been restored to the English throne, in 1660, only a fifth of the land belonged to the Catholic Irish families. Many of them had been sent to the poorer west of the country. There was more trouble when the Protestant Prince William of Orange was offered the throne of England in preference to the Catholic successor James II. The two contenders for the throne met at the Battle of the Boyne in 1690. James was defeated and a Protestant monarchy was

---

You can see Norman Ireland:

☞ at Trim Castle, County Meath;

☞ at Dublin Castle;

☞ at King John's Castle, Limerick; and

☞ in surnames such as Burke, Barry, Roche, Power, White, Fitzgerald and Butler.

guaranteed. The Ulster settlers in particular felt safer. Every summer throughout Northern Ireland the events of 1690 are commemorated by the descendants of those early settlers in parades and bonfires.

By the early 18th Century, although 75 per cent of the Irish population were Catholics, most of their ancestral lands were gone and harsh laws deprived them of many basic rights. School was illegal (just imagine) and many children attended classes hidden behind hedges or walls, called 'hedge schools'. A large number of Ulster Scots left for America and greater religious and political freedom. In late 18th-century France and America revolution was in the air, and it wasn't long before the Irish too were revolting! Fleets of French ships sent to support a rebellion in 1798 were unable to land and the attempted uprising failed.

In 1801 the Act of Union created the United Kingdom of Great Britain and Ireland, ruled from Westminster. From this point on, much of the story of Ireland revolves around an argument about this one Act. A majority of people came to reject it and demand that Ireland should rule itself. They would eventually be called nationalists. A large minority, concentrated in the northeastern part of Ireland, liked the Act of Union and wanted to leave it unchanged. They became known as unionists. The argument between these two groups became more bitter as the years passed. There was another uprising against British rule in 1916 by the nationalists, those who wanted an independent Irish state. Eventually, there was a compromise, which was agreed in 1921. The island of Ireland would be divided into two parts. The northeastern corner would remain part of the UK, while the rest would become an independent state.

This outcome did not satisfy everyone. Many nationalists who lived within the northeast, in what became known as Northern Ireland, rejected the agreement. There were periods of serious violence, which have only very recently come to an end. The Belfast Agreement in 1998 established a deal to share power between all sides, while respecting their different political views. Although this agreement hasn't solved all problems, it has improved life in Northern Ireland for very many people. The Nobel Peace Prize was awarded in 1976 to two ordinary women from Northern Ireland, and in 1998 to two leading politicians from the province, in recognition of their work for peace there.

Comings and goings, and the Celtic Tiger

The population of Ireland doubled in the first half of the 19th century, when it reached a record 8 million. By the end of the century the population had fallen by 50 per cent. The two things that caused this massive drop were famine and emigration. The diet of most people was based on the potato, which was usually plentiful, cheap and healthy. Sir Walter Raleigh had introduced it to his estates in Munster way back in 1596. Disaster struck when the entire potato crop failed in the period between 1845 and 1850. Around a million

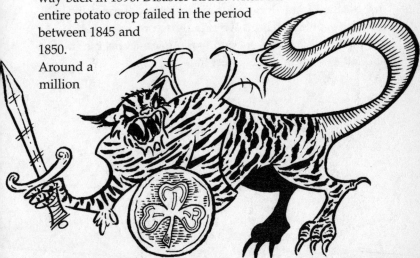

and a half people died of starvation. Emigration to Britain or further afield, to the United States, Canada and Australia, was the only option for those left standing. A million people in all left the island during the famine years. The fact that up to 40 million Americans have Irish ancestry, as well as millions of Canadians and Australians, is largely due to this one event.

Today the population is almost 4 million in the Republic, which is the highest it has been since 1871. It is growing faster than any other country in the European Union.

Twenty years ago only a tiny proportion of people from overseas lived in Ireland. Nowadays on the average Dublin bus you can hear people speaking languages from Asia, Africa and eastern Europe, as everyone chats on their mobile phones. In the six years up to 2002 well over half a million people entered the country. More than 277,600 were non-Irish. Even more were Irish people actually returning to live in their home country.

The economic boom of the 1990s lies behind these changes. The 'Celtic Tiger' is not something green and exotic that escaped from Dublin Zoo. The phrase describes the way the Irish economy has grown rapidly, to provide a high standard of living and enough work to attract people from abroad. And all in a very short time.

Local Customs: How the Irish Live

Family ties

In a recent survey of 111 countries around the world, Ireland topped the list as the best place to live. It scored high for its 'people skills' (rather than the weather!).

Irish families used to be quite big. At one time you would have trouble counting the number of cousins you had. There are now two children in the average family, but family ties are still strong. Most children call their mothers 'Mammy'. Many would say that Italian mothers and Irish mothers have a lot in common, because they are such central figures in the family.

The big family events revolve around births, christenings, weddings and funerals. These are often occasions when brothers, sisters and cousins, uncles, aunts and grandparents, and other relatives too, all get together. There is usually a good party to help things along. Although they don't always live with the family, as they did in the past, grandparents are important, often helping to mind younger children if both parents work.

As a lot of Irish people are Catholic, the day of their First Communion is a big day for many seven-year olds. Girls usually wear a white dress, which can sometimes be very elaborate, while boys get to look smarter than usual. They are often given presents of money. If an adult is described as still having their Communion money, it means they're slow to spend anything, and it isn't a compliment!

How's it going? Getting to know you

Irish people are generally quite easy-going. A good, firm handshake is important, although, for children, this might be a bit formal, so a smile is just perfect. People who know each other might well exchange a hug or a peck on the cheek, especially if they haven't seen each other for a while. The usual way of greeting people tends to involve talking more than touching.

Chatting for the sake of chatting is a chance to be sociable, not a waste of time. A sense of humour is highly appreciated, since, like people everywhere, the Irish enjoy a good laugh. You might notice that people often like to tease each other. It can be a bit startling if you're not used to it. This friendly teasing is sometimes called 'slagging' (not the same as 'slagging off', which is just being horrible!). If you can hold your own and give a good reply, you'll be fine. It's not unusual in Ireland to find that two people, who are themselves complete strangers, know someone in common. If the person they know happens to be famous, that's a plus, as it makes for a good story. Don't be surprised if people, especially older people, strike up a conversation on the bus or while standing in a queue.

People still salute strangers, especially in rural areas. Drivers might casually raise an index finger from the steering wheel by way of a 'hello'. In the cities things move faster, but you'll find that people are generally happy to help with directions or information.

Three Irish words you might come across are '*Fáilte*' (Welcome), '*Sláinte!*' (Cheers! Good health!) and '*Slán*' (Goodbye). You'll mostly see them written down, and people will enjoy telling you how to say them correctly.

Out and about in Irish towns

In general, the main street in an Irish town looks quite distinctive. There are banks and chain stores, but the many small shops and businesses give each town a different look. There are some things that you will notice are different, such as the post boxes, which are green in the Republic of Ireland and red in Northern Ireland. In the South road signs, street names, bus destinations and other public signs are almost always given in two languages, English and Irish.

You might need to ask directions from a *Garda* – a police officer. The Irish police are called the *Gardaí* and people also call them 'the guards'. Unlike continental police officers, they are not armed.

If you see a bus in Dublin with the destination 'An Lár', that's the one to hop on if you want to do some shopping. It goes right to the city centre. You might find more witches going to town to shop for underwear nowadays. There are fewer and fewer 'witches' knickers' (plastic bags) blowing around since the plastic bag charge was introduced in Irish supermarkets. People now pay 15 cents (about 10p) for those shopping bags that used to end up flapping in trees or telegraph wires. Good for the environment, chilly for witches!

No Irish town is complete without its pubs and you will rarely find one lone pub. Rather than having funny names like The Barmy Arms or historical ones like The Lamb and

Flag, you'll notice that the pubs
usually have someone's name on them, e.g.
O'Neills or Mulligan's. The pub as an actual
building is very important for giving directions to people,
especially in the cities. In Dublin some street corners are
actually called after the pubs located on them.

The Doors of Dublin

In the 18th century, Dublin was a prosperous Georgian city.
In 1757, the Wide Streets Commission redesigned entire
streets, broadening them and creating elegant squares for

wealthy citizens to enjoy. Granite slabs
were used to pave the footpaths and they
are still there, as are the brightly painted
doors. A door is a door, you might think,
but these Georgian doors were status
symbols, ways of letting people know that
the house-owner was important and
wealthy, and the doorways are what make each house
slightly different.

They have ornate doorknockers, some shaped like lions'
heads, others like a person's hand and often little fan-shaped
windows, called fanlights, overhead. Many of the fanlights
have beautiful teardrop or cobweb patterns.

Among the things you might spot as you travel through
parts of Ulster are coloured kerbstones and even lampposts.
In some towns these might be green, white and orange,
while in others they'll be red, white and blue. They show
that the people living in some places consider themselves to

be Irish, while those in others feel strongly that they are
British. In parts of Belfast you can see murals or wall
paintings on the sides of houses, depicting scenes from
distant and more recent history. They clearly identify which
tradition (Irish or British) the area belongs to.

In many smaller towns and villages throughout the island
the houses and shop fronts are painted in bright colours.
You'll see amazing combinations like mint green, pink,
yellow and lilac side by side.

On the road

One of the biggest changes south of the border is the amount
of road construction that has taken place in a short time.
Between 1995 and 2000 the total length of motorway in
Northern Ireland stood at 110km. During the same period
the Republic's motorways increased by 43 per cent, from
72km to 103km. Ireland's membership of the European
Union has been largely responsible for this increase.

In the Republic you won't see any 'Give Way' signs. Look
out for the 'Yield' signs instead.

Distances between places in the Republic are now
indicated in kilometres, though the older, prettier black-and-
white signs show miles. Speed limits in the Republic are also
indicated in kilometres. In Northern Ireland, both distances
and speeds are always shown in miles.

In the Republic you can tell which county a car has been
registered in because the letters are short for the county

name, usually the first and last letters of the word, e.g. WW (Wicklow), KY (Kerry), MO (Mayo). The main cities have one initial. Guess where D, C, G and L cars come from?

D'telly

The Irish telly addict has a good range of TV channels to choose from. There are four Irish TV stations. RTÉ 1 (Radio Telefís Éireann) and RTÉ 2, both state-owned, show ads, but viewers also pay for TV licences. TV3 is a commercial station and TG4 broadcasts programmes in Irish and English. Viewers can also get the British channels BBC1 (Northern Ireland), BBC2, Channel 4 and Ulster Television (part of ITV).

The Late Late Show, first broadcast in 1962, is the world's longest-running chat show. It was presented by Gay Byrne (a very famous figure in Ireland) until 1999 when Pat Kenny took over. It is an Irish institution, which has debated important issues in Ireland and has featured both celebrities and ordinary people from Ireland and abroad. A regular favourite is the Toy Show which presents some of the amazing toys that people can buy around Christmas time.

As well as international favourites, such as *The Simpsons*, *Friends* or *Neighbours*, there are a number of popular Irish children's programmes. One of these is *The Den*, with Dustin the Turkey, who looks more like a vulture than a turkey. Dustin's best-selling album is *Dustin Unplucked*. He is a close friend of Zig and Zag, who made zogabongs a fashion item in the 1990s and went on to become *Big Breakfast* stars after their TV debut on RTÉ.

Far and away...

About a million Irish-born people live outside Ireland. You will sometimes hear them talk about 'at home', 'going home' meaning 'in Ireland' or 'going back to Ireland', even though they don't actually live there! It doesn't mean that they are homesick or bonkers, just that they stay in touch. About 70 million people around the world can claim Irish roots. Did you know that at least 13 of the 42 US Presidents have been of Irish descent?

People still regularly leave to work all over the world, but nowadays they usually choose to go. Every year the airports are packed with people welcoming their family members 'home' for Christmas. Coming and going has never been easier because there are now direct flights from Ireland to most places in the world.

... and away with the fairies

Everyone's heard of leprechauns. In fact, they're so famous that most people don't have problems pronouncing their name! But there's a lot more to Irish folklore than the gnarly little shoemakers.

Before information and knowledge was as freely available as it is today, people believed strongly in good and bad luck

Did you know...

... there's an Ireland in the USA?

There are **Dublins** in: New Hampshire, Pennsylvania, Maryland, Virginia, Indiana, Ohio, Georgia, Texas and California!

You can also find other Irish place names in the USA: **Belfast** (Maine), **Derry** (New Mexico, New Hampshire), **Dingle** (Idaho), **Tyrone** (New Mexico and Kansas) and of course there's Ireland... in Texas.

and were often superstitious. An Irish superstitious custom is still called a *piseóg*. For example, if a person lost something, the fairies might be up to mischief. The person would 'lock in the fairies' by crossing two twigs and placing a stone on top. If the missing object then turned up, the fairies could be released again.

A field with the remains of a fort or a stone circle would be treated with particular caution, as these landmarks were associated with the fairies. To stay in their good books people would go to great lengths to avoid disturbing a 'fairy fort' or 'fairy circle'.

When unusual things occurred in the natural

environment, the fairies were also thought to be busy. A sudden mini-whirlwind lasting only seconds was called a 'fairy wind'. People believed that the real world and the invisible world of the fairies were very close. At certain times of the year, such as Hallowe'en, it was even possible for the spirits to cross over from one world to the other.

In folklore, if you caught a leprechaun, you couldn't take your eyes off him or he'd vanish in an instant. He would promise to lead you to his pot of gold, hidden at the foot of the rainbow, but then would usually wangle his way out of it.

The *Púca* (pooka) is the scary fairy. Children would avoid picking blackberries late in the season because the *Púca* would have beaten them to it and left 'spit' on the berries. He would appear as a dark horse with yellow eyes and a long black mane. He could also be a goblin, a hairy bogeyman or a goat. However he looked, he went out and about at night, and was usually up to no good.

The *bean-sídhe* (ban shee) turned up at night and her wailing meant that someone was about to die.

Originally this fairy woman only dealt with a select few Irish families. A spooky fairy who wails like… a banshee!

Not so long ago, when a person died the family would have a wake. The body would stay at home, rather than be taken to a funeral parlour. The clock in the house would be stopped at the time of death and it would stay that way until after the burial. Then the wake would begin. People prayed, but also sang songs, told stories and played games all night. Despite the sadness, the wake was a very sociable occasion and a celebration of the person's life. Even though the custom has changed in most places, it is still a matter of great family pride to show hospitality to people coming to sympathize. It is important, too, to give the dead person 'a good send-off'.

The places where these customs were strongest were often badly affected by emigration. Many traditions simply died out.

Children often have to ask their grandparents to tell them stories of how things used to be. It's usually thanks to children that some of the traditions have survived or are being revived.

Ah go on, tell us a story!

The art of storytelling has been around a very long time. People used to gather to tell each other stories, share food, and round off the evening with some music and dancing. The storyteller or seanchaí

42

was
a key figure who
would liven up the long
winter evenings with scary or
entertaining tales. There are
storytelling gatherings today, especially in Wexford.

Hallowe'en

Long before the pumpkins and the skeletons, Hallowe'en
was celebrated by Celtic peoples as Samhain, the end of the
old year. In fact, the word 'Samhain' is still the Irish word for
November. With Christianity the pagan festival also became
linked with the period around All Souls Day, 2 November,
when people remember their dead relatives. The Celts
believed that this was a time when their world and the spirit
world were so close that it was possible for spirits to 'cross
over'. So all those spooky witches, ghouls and Grim Reapers
have a very long tradition behind them. In Ireland children
have always visited houses collecting fruit, nuts, sweets or
money. With the influence of telly, they might say 'Trick or
Treat', but they might also say (especially in Dublin), 'Help
the Hallowe'en party.'

Although not traditionally a feature of Hallowe'en,
fireworks are now very common all over Ireland. You can't
buy them easily south of the border but there are always
plenty about. In Northern Ireland, they can be bought if you
have a licence. Dubliners, however, have been able to buy

them in the most unlikely places. Once you would have found them among the cabbages and chrysanthemums of the street markets. 'D'ye want some bangers or rockets, love?' the fruit and veg seller might ask, keeping a wary eye out for the *Gardaí*. She would then magic a large rocket or a fat Roman candle from under her apron!

Christmas

Irish Christmas traditions are now similar to those elsewhere – Christmas trees, the crib, decorations and fairy lights everywhere. One practice in particular goes back a long time. A single candle is often placed in the window of the house. This is a sign that the house would welcome any wanderer in search of a place to stay, and also a reminder of Joseph and Mary, who weren't so lucky.

The 'Wran'

On 26 December, which is always called St Stephen's Day in Ireland, a tradition that was once widespread, and is now being revived in parts of the country, is the hunt for the 'Wran' (the wren). The story is that as St Stephen, a Christian martyr killed in AD 34, was hiding from his pursuers, a wren rustled in the ivy, giving away his hiding place. So groups of boys called Wrenboys get together to hunt the wren and punish him. In the past a real wren would be caught and killed. The poor thing would then be paraded from house to house, while the boys, disguised in colourful costumes and masks, would dance around chanting rhymes. The Wrenboys would ask for food or drink in return for their entertainment. Luckily, the bird is no longer killed and the modern 'Wran' is more like street theatre.

Mummers, rhymers and strawboys

Like the Wrenboys, mummers disguise themselves, often in straw costumes and high-pointed straw hats. They dance, sing and perform plays with characters called Jenny Wren, Jack Straw, St George, St Patrick, the Turkish Knight, the Doctor with his bag of tricks and (would you believe it?) Oliver Cromwell. The audience gets to boo and hiss every time he shows up! Mumming is popular in Wexford in the southeast, as well as north of the border. There, the tradition is said to be about 2,500 years old and mummers are thought to have entertained the ancient Ulster court. They are also known there as rhymers. They are popular as fund-raisers and they visit local pubs collecting money for charity in exchange for some lively entertainment. Some folk theatre groups, such as the Armagh Rhymers, perform mini-dramas on various themes and

visit schools, inviting children to act out the plots of their stories.

Strawboys are usually found in the west of Ireland. Their speciality is to entertain at weddings. Weddings used to be celebrated at the bride's home, so the wedding party was usually quite small. Those who were not invited would be highly offended. They would gatecrash the party, usually disguised in straw costumes. The strawboys would play instruments and entertain people so that they would be allowed to stay. They usually brought along a rich old man to dance with the bride and a wise old lady to dance with the groom. These would guarantee good fortune and a long life. Today strawboys are invited to many weddings in the west of Ireland as a surprise for the couple.

A School Day in Ireland

School daze

About 40 per cent of the people in the Republic of Ireland
are under the age of 25, so most days about a quarter of the
Irish population is sitting in a classroom! Children
throughout Ireland can start school from the age of four and
generally move up to secondary school at 12.

Primary school children spend at least 183 days at school.
For 56 days in the year, including the whole of July and
August, they're on holiday! There are at least 167 days in the
secondary school year, but schools close from early June until
September for most students. They also have mid-term breaks,
as well as Christmas and Easter holidays. All children in the
South have a Bank Holiday weekend around Hallowe'en.

Generally, children have packed lunches. The average
lunch break in primary schools is about half an hour, and the
whole day lasts just over five and a half hours. Secondary
school days are longer, but most finish before 4 pm.

School uniforms are very common throughout Ireland.
Limerick has the record for the longest uniform skirts.
They reach down almost to the ankles and the girls think it's
quite cool!

Gaeilge/Irish

Though English is the main language used throughout the
country, all children in the South and many in the North

study Irish at school. In primary schools children usually have two versions of their name, one English and the other Irish. Surnames in Irish change depending on whether a person is male or female. Ronan Murphy would become Rónán Ó Murchú, while Una Murphy would become Úna Ní Mhurchú. 'Ó' means 'son of' and 'Ní' means 'daughter of'. However, if your surname is of Norman origin, it doesn't change in this way. For instance, the names 'Brown' and 'Power' are translated as 'de Brún' and 'de Paor'. Can you spot the French connection?

More and more children all over the island go to Irish-speaking schools, or *gaelscoileanna*. There are 181 of these, and 149 of them are primary schools. The children in a gaelscoil study everything through Irish, even maths and science! Many Irish teenagers go to summer colleges in the Gaeltacht areas and stay with local Irish-speaking families. They spend a month practising their Irish in classes. There's lots of sports, music and socialising too. As for continental languages, Irish students study French, German, Spanish and Italian, in that order.

Hard work

A survey carried out in 2004 showed that girls spend, on average, about 12 hours a week on homework, while boys spend nine hours on it. A very large number of Irish students (about 70 per cent in the survey) take 'grinds' (private lessons) outside school hours, mostly in maths, French, English and Irish.

The Junior Certificate is the first state exam for 14/15-year-olds in the South. Like students in England and Wales, students from Northern Ireland take GCSEs.

In the Republic a very large number of pupils stay on at school right up to the age of 17 or 18 and take between five and eight subjects in the Leaving Certificate exams.

In Northern Ireland, A-level students specialize in three subjects.

Hard cash

Parents in the South buy all their children's school books. Many people exchange or buy used books online, or they simply rent them in order to save money.

The highlight for many students at the end of their school careers in the South is the Debs' Ball. It can cost a fortune for some parents, who pay for tickets, dress hire and even stretch limousines!

We love boffins!

Dublin's annual Young Scientists' Exhibition celebrated its 40th birthday in 2004, when 1,040 students (719 girls and 321 boys) from the whole of Ireland took part. The very first winner of the competition, in 1965, went on to run a biotechnology company in the US!

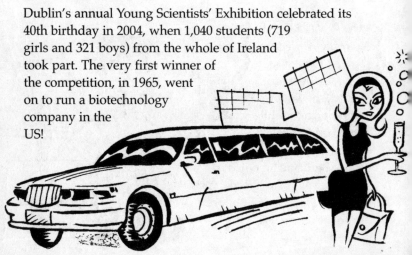

Fabulous Buildings and Sights

The Dublin Spire, Dublin City

In July 2003 the Spire of Dublin was officially inaugurated on the main street of Dublin, which is called O'Connell Street. Rising from a 3-metre base and tapering to a 15-centimetre tip, it's considered to be among the tallest sculptures in the world, at a height of 120 metres (393 feet). Often the upper part disappears into cloud and it's designed to sway in the wind, but just enough to be safe! Inevitably this hard-to-ignore monument caused a good deal of argument. Constructed in three phases, using huge chunks of rolled stainless steel, the Spire was the result of a competition to design a Dublin landmark suited to the 21st century.

It has a hard act to follow, since the site was formerly occupied by Admiral Lord Nelson on top of his pillar. Nelson's Pillar stood in the heart of Dublin for 157 years and was a favourite meeting place for Dubliners. It was 134 feet and 5 inches high, and was situated opposite the General Post Office. In March 1966 Nelson's Pillar was blown up, exactly 50 years after the historic uprising of 1916. Apart from poor old Nelson's head, which can now be seen at Dublin's Civic Museum, nothing remains of the pillar. The exact spot remained vacant for 37 years until the ultra-modern Spire arrived.

Dubliners have had an absolute ball inventing nicknames for the Spire. They called it the Stiletto in the Ghetto, the

Why in the Sky, the Nail in the Pale and the Eyeful Tower, and now it's known as 'the Spike'. Ouch. But you get the feeling that it will grow on them.

The Giant's Causeway, County Antrim

These black volcanic rock and cliff formations are Northern Ireland's most popular visitor destination, and the area is a UNESCO World Heritage Site. When you see the 40,000-odd hexagonal columns rising up from the Antrim coast, you can well imagine that people wondered how they had come about.

In the late 17th century the site became a subject of great interest to scientists. People wondered whether the columns had been painstakingly carved by humans, or if they were simply one of nature's wonders. Then, of course, there was the giant who gave the rocks their name. Finn McCool was a mighty Ulster warrior with more legends to

his name than you've had hot dinners. In one story, Finn had
a rival called Benandonner, who lived in nearby Scotland.
The causeway was supposed to bridge the narrow sea
between the two countries. In the end neither giant was
comfortable with the thought that the other could easily step
across into his territory. As the Scottish giant was
considerably beefier, Finn decided to rip up the columns
nearest the coast of Scotland, to keep Benandonner at a safe
distance.

In fact, 60 million years ago massive volcanic eruptions
occurred in this part of Antrim. Tons of molten rock were
forced up through gaps in the chalk bed, to form a series of
lava formations. The distinctive black volcanic rock is called
basalt. The molten rock cooled at different rates before
hardening into the tightly packed pillars that you can see
today. Some of them are up to 40 feet high. The nuggets of
basalt embedded in the nearby cliffs are called 'giant's eyes'.
There's the Giant's Harp, layers of rock standing almost

upright like a stringed instrument. After climbing the columns, you can sit in the Giant's Boot, which is a bit like a comfortable but rock-solid bean bag!

The Burren, County Clare

The Burren is Ireland's answer to the lunar landscape. It gets its name from the Irish word *boireann*, meaning 'stony district'. That is exactly what it is – more than 500 square miles of limestone pavement, crisscrossed by deep cracks between the slabs of rock. The limestone was formed 360 million years ago, under warm seas (hard to imagine on a wet, windy day!). The seabed was gradually pushed upwards and glaciers stripped the surface to form a vast rocky plateau. Cromwell's soldiers called it a place where you couldn't drown, hang or bury a man! It's mysterious, hiding underground caves and rivers that swell with rainwater. When these rivers flood, lakes called turloughs start to appear above ground, but they disappear again as the waters ebb away. If this were a desert, they'd be mirages.

But the Burren isn't barren. It's more of a gigantic rock garden with a unique plant life. Plants that are normally found in places as far apart as the Arctic and the Mediterranean grow side by side here in the mild climate, and specialists go wild about them.

If you're not into rock gardens, there are lots of stone-age tombs and megalithic forts to spark your imagination about the people who inhabited the area thousands of years ago. The eerie dolmen at Poulnabrone dates back to between 3800 and 3200 BC. When it was excavated in 1986, the remains of about 22 people, including six children, were found in this burial place. Spookier still is the Ailwee Cave, which is another of the Burren's mysteries. It was discovered in 1944 by a local farmer, whose dog was chasing rabbits! The cave cuts a third of a mile into the heart of the limestone mountain. It hasn't changed in size since Ireland lay under glaciers about 10,000 years ago. It is clear from animal skeletons that the cave was used by bears, who scraped out shallow pits so that they could hibernate there.

Blarney Castle, County Cork

The castle at Blarney was a stronghold of the McCarthy family and was built in 1446. Today all that's left of the original building is the castle keep. With its narrow slits for windows and its battlements, Blarney Castle was one of the strongest fortresses in the whole of Munster. The story goes that this strong position allowed the 16th-century owner, Cormac McCarthy, to delay handing the castle over to Sir George Carew. Carew demanded the castle in the name of his Queen, Elizabeth I. McCarthy managed to put things off by inventing all sorts of excuses not to move out. All the while he remained perfectly pleasant and polite. It is said that Elizabeth was really not impressed and dismissed all these fine words as so much 'blarney' and, hey presto, a new word was born. In the end she got her way.

Every year thousands of people visit the castle to kiss the Blarney Stone. No one really knows where this peculiar custom came from, though it began some time in the 19th century. That adds up to quite a lot of germs when you think about it, so what makes people so keen to do it? First, there's the challenge of actually getting right to the top of the keep where the large stone is located. As it's set in the wall just below the battlements, you then have to lean backwards, holding onto two hand rails. You really have to trust the guide, who hangs on to you by the legs so that you don't drop head first to the ground, 126 feet below! Once you've kissed the stone, you're supposed to receive the 'gift of the gab', the ability to speak with great eloquence. It's hard to prove whether this really works, especially if you're already chatty, but it does show that you've got a head for heights and a steady nerve!

Slieve League Cliffs, County Donegal

On the west coast of Ireland's most northerly county, the marine cliffs at Slieve League are said to be the highest in Europe. The cliffs extend along the coast for about 3 km and the sheer 603-metre drop into the Atlantic is stunning but scary, especially on a windy day. The route leading to the main sightseeing spot, known as the 'big view', is a hair-raising ride all on its own and, at eight kilometres, it lasts longer than any roller coaster. Just about wide enough for cars to pass each other, the road snakes upwards in a series of hairpin bends. At the brow of each hill the jagged cliff tops begin to come into view. Experienced climbers can climb to the top of Slieve League itself by a route called One Man's Pass, but most people are happy with the view you get over the whole of Donegal Bay. In the early 19th century, a watchtower was built to warn of possible attacks from the sea by Napoleon's forces. Ireland's coastline is dotted with these watchtowers because the threat of attack by the French from the west was very real to 19th-century England.

Ulster American Folk Park, County Tyrone

Founded in 1976 to celebrate 200 years of American independence, and the links between Ulster and the US, the Folk Park tells the story of the two million Ulster people who left their homes to start new lives in America during the 18th and 19th centuries. It is Europe's largest museum of emigration, and traces the lives of some of the famous and not-so-famous emigrants. No less than ten American presidents can trace their roots back to this small province and the man responsible for printing the American Declaration of Independence was also an Ulsterman. John Joseph Hughes, founder of St Patrick's Cathedral on New York's Fifth Avenue, came from County Tyrone. Many of the early emigrants were pioneers who became known in America as the Scotch-Irish because they brought with them their Scottish Presbyterian religion and culture. Some of these new Americans went on to achieve great things, especially in business.

Much of what can be seen in the Folk Park is based on the life story of one man, Judge Thomas Mellon. Mellon left home as a five-year-old boy, settled in Pennysylvania, and went on to make his fortune in industry and the railways. Homes like his in Ulster have been reconstructed in great detail. Everyday life and typical activities like weaving, baking and candle-making are shown and visitors can have a go at these skills.

The story of the waves of not-so-famous emigrants forced to leave Ulster and the island of Ireland in general during the famine years of the 19th century is also told. A million and a half of these desperate people found work in the big industrial cities of the eastern US. Their living conditions are recreated in the museum and they were often grim. Visitors can even board a full-scale replica of a cramped and creaking emigrant ship to sail to the New World. Some of the ships, known as 'coffin ships', weren't seaworthy and never made it to America.

Newgrange, Brú na Bóinne, County Meath

Ireland's oldest and most visited prehistoric building is located near the High Kings' ancient capital of Tara. The megalithic tomb at Newgrange was built between 3500 and 2700 BC. That makes it 500 years older than the Egyptian

Pyramids and 1,500 years older than Stonehenge. It is part of a complex of burial sites known as the Boyne cemetery and is a UNESCO World Heritage Site. Together these sites attract almost a quarter of a million visitors every year.

Newgrange is an enormous burial chamber called a passage grave, originally surrounded by huge upright boulders (up to eight feet high), many of which are still standing today. The overall diameter of the original Great Circle of stones (106.3 metres) was greater than that of Stonehenge (97.5 metres). At the entrance to the tomb lie large boulders with amazing patterns of spirals, zigzags, circles and triangles carefully carved into the rock. Some of the patterns are thought to represent the Sun, the Moon and human faces. Some archeologists say that the curving patterns make the massive boulders appear even larger and that this was a deliberate stone-age optical illusion. Inside the chamber, the stone slabs of the ceiling have been constructed so that not a single drop of Irish rain was able to enter the chamber in 5,000 years. The mind boggles!

Newgrange had great ceremonial significance, especially at the time of the winter solstice, when the days are at their shortest. The stone-age architects of the tomb were well aware of the solstice when they built it. At dawn a narrow slit in the roof near the entrance to the tomb allows a single ray of winter sun to light up the passageway leading into the central chamber. As the sun rises, the chamber is gradually flooded with a golden light. The whole amazing event lasts about 17 minutes. Archeologists have worked out that the building was constructed so that the ray of sunlight would enter the tomb with the accuracy of a laser beam and that it would last as long as possible. This event would be most likely to occur for about three days around the 21 December. Ten people are able to witness this annual event at first hand by entering a lottery in October. In 2003 20,000 people entered the lottery for the chance to catch a glimpse.

Doing Dublin

Dublin, the capital city of the Republic of Ireland, is...

laid-back

historic

Dublin Castle

Ha'penny Bridge

relaxing

St Stephen's Green

beautiful

River Liffey

impressive

O'Connell Statue

surprising

Dublin Spire

...but best of all, it's buzzing!

Temple Bar

It's great!

Inventors, Writers, Rebels and Good Guys... and a Rake

Voyages of discovery

St Brendan was one of the many monks who established monasteries around Ireland before setting off on their travels as Christian missionaries. Brendan was born some time in the 6th century. He may have sailed as far as North America, according to a 9th-century manuscript known as *The Voyage*. This manuscript describes Brendan as having visions of the Promised Land across the Atlantic. With a small crew of monks he set off on a seven-year voyage and is thought to have reached Iceland, Greenland and finally the coast of North America. *The Voyage* also tells of meetings with St Patrick, who lived and died long before, and some narrow escapes from sea monsters, so it's not always easy to separate fact from fiction. Anyway, how could a few monks in a little boat tackle those huge Atlantic waves and live to tell the tale? In 1976 a British explorer, Tim Severin, built a little circular boat, modelling it on a 6th-century craft called a coracle. The coracle was made of waterproofed leather stretched over a wooden frame. (Fishermen in the west of

64

Ireland still use something similar, which they call a *currach*.) Tim Severin and his crew travelled from the western Aran Islands and Donegal northwards to the Hebrides, the Faroe Islands, Iceland and onwards to North America. His amazing experiment proved that it would certainly have been possible for Irish monks to do the same. You can see Tim Severin's coracle known as the Brendan Boat at Craggaunowen in County Clare.

Robert Boyle (1627–91) was born at Lismore Castle in County Waterford, the son of the 1st Earl of Cork, Richard Boyle. Richard Boyle was very much involved in all sorts of political intrigues at court in London, but managed to stay in royal favour long enough to become the first colonial millionaire. Robert was one of his 14 children. He was sent away to Eton at just eight years of age and then went to Oxford to follow a scientific career. He is known as the father of chemistry because of his huge influence on a science that was still very new. He established the importance of the experimental method, a way of working on which the whole of modern science is based. His experiments with the vacuum pump showed that in a vacuum sound cannot be heard, a feather falls faster than it does in air, a candle cannot stay alight and animals cannot survive. Boyle's Law, for which he is most famous, states that, at a constant temperature, the volume of gas is in inverse proportion to the pressure applied to it. Go figure.

John Barry (1745–1803) was born in County Wexford. He was the son of a farmer and went to sea as a cabin boy while he was still a teenager. He became master of a merchant ship and was given a naval commission early in the American War of Independence. The first English warship to be captured by the American navy in 1776 was taken by Barry, who was in command of the Lexington. He won many more naval victories and eventually became a commodore. Barry wrote a book that set out a code of signals allowing ships to communicate with each other when they were sailing in squadrons. He also trained many young naval officers who went on to distinguish themselves in battle. He earned the title of 'Father of the American Navy' in recognition of all his achievements. The town of Wexford honours him with a statue which was presented to the Irish people by US President Eisenhower in 1956.

William Rowan Hamilton (1805–65) was born in Dublin and educated by his uncle, a clergyman. William was a genuinely bright spark with a good knowledge of some modern languages as well as Latin and Greek by the age of 12. He also taught himself mathematics. He was still a junior university student when he was appointed a professor of astronomy. He went on to become a member of all the major scientific academies of Europe and was knighted in 1835. He discovered the quaternion. That sounds like something from *The Lord of the Rings*, but in fact it's a type of mathematical formula that is still used in the creation of computer games and in flight simulators.

John Tyndall (1820–93) was a physicist, born in County Carlow, who was working at the Royal Institution of Great Britain in London in 1854. He studied meteorology, the science of weather formation. He was also a pioneer in the study of bacterial infections and the means of curing them. He invented the fibre optic, now found in those twinkling fibre-optic lamps and artificial Christmas trees. He was fascinated by glaciers and his work involved a lot of mountain-climbing, which he loved. He gave his name to a number of mountain peaks around the world. He also gave his name to the scattering of light that gives the sky its colour. What scientists now call the Tyndall effect answers the question 'Why is the sky blue?'.

Harry Ferguson (1884–1960) was born near Hillsborough in County Down and was involved with all sorts of motors from very early on. He raced motorcycles and cars, and in

1909
he
made
the first
flight in Ireland.
He managed to build his own plane
using plans that he found in a magazine. (Don't try that at home.) His greatest contribution was to help farmers to plough their fields using a combined tractor and plough. Before this invention, ploughing with a horse-drawn plough was a tough, slow method of doing an essential farming job. In 1938 Ferguson agreed that the American motor giant Ford would manufacture his ploughs. The mechanized plough contributed hugely to food production during wartime. Working together with a Canadian company, Massey, Ferguson was responsible for the Massey–Ferguson tractor.

Wordsmiths and their words

One of the things you'll notice when you arrive in Ireland are the many photos and posters of writers displayed in airports, bookshops and cafés. Ireland produces writers of every kind and always has done.

Jonathan Swift (1667–1745) was a Protestant clergyman born and educated in Dublin.

He gave children the fantastic tales of *Gulliver's Travels* and adults the word Yahoo, which you still hear being used

in Ireland to describe a rude or ignorant person. After a successful career in England, he was sent back to Dublin in 1713 to take up a position as the Dean of St Patrick's Cathedral. He used his skills as a writer to attack the hypocrisy and injustice that he saw around him. This he did by making fun of those he saw as responsible for a lot of the damage. Sometimes he used shock tactics. In one essay, 'A Modest Proposal', he proposes a solution to the problem of poverty and hunger among the Irish poor: let them eat their own children (and while you're at it, here are some recipes). It caused a huge uproar. In *Gulliver's Travels* (1726) the hero Lemuel Gulliver travels to a number of strange lands, including Lilliput, where the people are tiny and he is a giant. Then it's on to Brobdingnag, the land of giants, where it's exactly the reverse. Gulliver's last port of call is a land where horses are the sensible creatures and rule the Yahoos, who look like human beings but have no clothes or language. In 1988, as part of Dublin's celebrations of its 1,000 years as a city, a 20-

metre long model of Gulliver was washed up on a Dublin beach. If you want to know what that says about the inhabitants of the island he ended up on, you'll just have to read the book!

Bram Stoker (1847–1912) was a Dublin-born writer of strange and seriously creepy tales. His most famous gothic novel is *Dracula*, which has inspired lots of horror films. Count Dracula, a vampire from Transylvania, tries to invade England and the novel tells of the various attempts to foil him before he sinks his fangs into any more innocent travellers. Anyone seen the garlic?

James Joyce (1882–1941) was also born and brought up in Dublin, though he spent much of his life abroad and eventually died in Zurich in Switzerland. His family was poor and moved house a lot. In all, Joyce may have changed address more than 20 times. He left Ireland in 1904 with a Galway woman called Nora Barnacle. With typical Dublin wit, Joyce's father remarked that, with a name like that, she was bound to stick to him. Joyce was frustrated by life in a city that he found stuffy and depressing. Yet Dublin is very much at the centre of his works. He wrote a collection of short stories called *Dubliners*, which

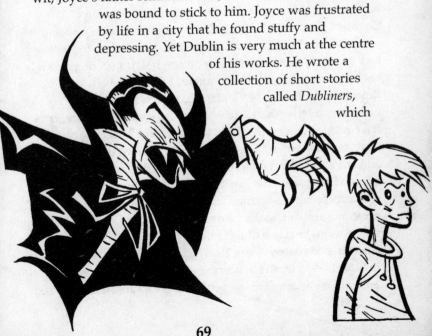

depicts the lives of ordinary people, young and old. His most famous novel is called *Ulysses* (mispronounced by some people as Useless). The hero of the novel is not the ancient Greek voyager but a Dubliner, Leopold Bloom. The book describes Bloom's 'voyage' through the city on a single day, 16 June 1904. Dublin's River Liffey is another of Joyce's heroes. In *Finnegans Wake* the first word of what is probably the most difficult book to read in the English language is 'riverrun'. (After that, it gets really complicated.) The word describes the Liffey as it flows through the city into Dublin Bay. Dublin now has a fountain with a bronze statue of Joyce's river heroine, Anna Livia, as a woman with long streaming hair, lying back as the waters flow over her. She was quickly nicknamed 'the floozie in the jacuzzi'. The 'floozie' had to be moved to make way for the 'Spike', the new Millennium Spire, which arrived in 2003. Hopefully she won't have to move 20 times like poor old James Joyce. Joyce was a talented singer and he was also the manager of the first cinema to be opened in Dublin, called the Volta.

Samuel Beckett (1906–89), was another Dublin writer who reworked the English language so much that, in 1969, he won the Nobel Prize for Literature. Beckett spent much of his time in France and even worked for the French Resistance between 1941 and 1942, narrowly escaping discovery by the Nazis. He was awarded the great honour of the Croix de Guerre (Military Cross) by the French for his resistance activities. He eventually chose to write in French, and some of his most famous work was first published in his adopted language. His strange plays sometimes feature odd characters, such as couples in dustbins or buried up to their necks in sand, always waiting for something to happen or trying to make sense of their lives. Hmm.

Seamus Heaney (born 1939) is a poet from County Derry in Northern Ireland. He was the eldest of nine children and grew up on a farm. He has achieved great fame as a poet and a scholar, teaching at Harvard and at Oxford as well as in his native Ireland. He remembers that, as a child, he watched American soldiers who were stationed near his home preparing for the Normandy landings of the Second World War. He felt then that history was being made right before his eyes. He has always been fascinated by the past. He has also written about Northern Ireland and its troubled history. He is best known for his poems about the simple things in nature and daily life. He won the Nobel Prize for Literature in 1995. When he was told the big news, the gobsmacked poet handed the phone to his wife. He explained later: 'You cannot possibly speak a sentence that begins, "I have won the Nobel Prize." That would be scandalous.'

Roddy Doyle (born 1958) taught English at a secondary school in north Dublin until he decided to become a full-time writer. He has written four books for children, including *The Giggler Treatment* and *The Meanwhile Adventures*. His very funny novels about life in a fictional Dublin working-class suburb called Barrytown have been hugely successful. They are perfect for cinema and television: the best-known film adaptation is Alan Parker's *The Commitments*. In 1993 Doyle won the Booker Prize for *Paddy Clarke Ha Ha Ha*, about the life and times of a schoolboy growing up. One of Doyle's ex-pupils complimented him on his first big novel saying, 'It's the best book I ever read'. He then added, 'It's the only book I ever read.'

Feisty women and rebel hearts

Grace O'Malley (c.1530–1603) was an Irish pirate queen who ruled the waves off the west coast of Ireland during the reign of Elizabeth I. Married twice to members of powerful Irish families, Grace was famous in her own right as a strong, daring leader and an able seawoman. She constantly

challenged the authority of the crown in western Connacht by demanding taxes from all ships passing through her territory. The Lord Deputy of Ireland, Sir Henry Sidney, was mightily impressed by her abilities as a sea captain. One story tells how Grace was so fearsome that she left a sea battle to give birth below deck. Once her son was born, she went straight back up to finish (and win) the battle. Her life on the wrong side of the law meant spells in prison and even a narrow escape from the gallows. She is said to have gone to see Queen Elizabeth in person in 1593 to petition her for lands for herself and her son. It seems to have worked. However, she later joined in a rebellion against Elizabeth and fled to Ulster. Although she was pardoned by Elizabeth, she lost her ships and with them her wealth.

Maud Gonne McBride (1865–1953) was born to a British army officer of Irish descent and an English mother, and moved to Ireland when her father was posted to Dublin in 1882. She became a strong supporter of the Irish struggle for independence and ended a relationship with a French lover when she discovered that he didn't feel the same way. She founded a women's revolutionary movement. A famous beauty in her day, with a taste for fine clothes, Maud was described as incredibly elegant, with the walk of a queen. She organized a party for 30,000 schoolchildren that just happened to clash with an official visit to Ireland by Queen Victoria. Her party meant that there were fewer children to wave flags in the streets for the royal visitor! The Nobel Prize-winning poet W. B. Yeats was madly in love with her and proposed marriage many times, but she always turned him down. Instead, she married a fellow revolutionary, John MacBride, in 1903. The marriage didn't work and they parted. Like many people of the time, she was very much against the Anglo-Irish Treaty of 1921, which brought the war of independence between Britain and Ireland to an end.

All-round good guys... and a rake

Arthur Guinness (1725–1803) began a great family of brewers. In 1752 Arthur inherited £100 and started his first brewery in Leixlip, County Kildare. In 1759 he moved to a disused brewery at St James's Gate in Dublin. In 1775 he had a row with Dublin Corporation, which accused him of using more than the legal amount of free water to make his beer. Guinness was prepared to fight off the sheriff with a pickaxe in order to defend the water supply. In 1778 he began to brew stout, a dark beer containing roasted barley. It was popular with London porters. Guinness's son, also called Arthur, took over in 1803. The family's beer, which became known as 'extra stout porter', sold well, especially during the early 19th century, and the St James's Gate brewery became the largest exporter of stout in the world. It still is today. Every day around 10 million glasses of stout are consumed worldwide. In 1951 while shooting game in County Wexford, the managing director of the brewing company now known as Arthur Guinness, Son & Co. Ltd wanted to settle an argument about the fastest European game bird. It occurred to him that a book with this kind of information would be a good idea. Four years later the first *Guinness Book of Records* was published.

Thomas 'Buck' Whaley (1766–1800) had a gambling problem from day one. At 13 he inherited £7,000 a year (a fortune in those days), lands in County Wicklow and the fine house on Dublin's Stephen's Green where he was born. When he went to study in Paris at 16 he managed to gamble away £14,000 in a single night and was sent back home in disgrace. Desperate for cash, he accepted a bet that he would walk to Jerusalem, play ball against the walls of the city and come back in one piece within two years. Seven thousand miles later and well within the time limit, he returned to collect his £20,000. The money didn't last and during his time as an MP in the old Irish Parliament he managed to vote in favour of the 1801 Act of Union with Great Britain and, later, against the very same Act… each time for a good sum of money, of course! The Dublin rake has a pub named after him.

Thomas John Barnardo (1845–1905) was born in Dublin into a wealthy background, but he became deeply religious and decided to dedicate his life to helping the poor. While training to be a medical missionary to China, he was shocked at the thousands of homeless boys he found sleeping rough in London's East End. He founded the first Dr Barnardo's Home in 1870 and vowed never to close the door to any child needing shelter. By 1900 up to 8,000 children were being cared for thanks to his efforts. Although it is 30 years since Barnardo's ran orphanages, the organization continues its work with children and young people today.

Mary Robinson (born 1944) was born in County Mayo. Her parents were both doctors. She studied law at university and became a professor of law at 25. After a successful legal career, involving many cases both in Ireland and in the European courts, she was elected to the Irish Senate, or Seanad, in 1969 and her political career took off. She was elected as the first woman President of Ireland in 1990. Her victory was seen as evidence that the Republic's increasingly young voters wanted to see major changes in their country. She was Ireland's most active President, travelling to places struck by famine or war. In 1996 she became the first Irish President ever to pay an official visit to Britain, where she met Queen Elizabeth II at Buckingham Palace. This was a significant gesture of friendship in the hard work needed to build a peaceful future for Northern Ireland. From 1997 to 2002 she was United Nations High Commissioner for Human Rights, and continued to work for people's social, economic and cultural rights.

Thomas 'Buck' Whaley

75

Food and Drink

*'Yum, yum, pig's bum,
Cabbage and potatoes.'*

This Irish children's rhyme describes one of the best-known traditional Irish dishes – bacon and cabbage accompanied by potatoes. It's not exactly exotic but it's hearty and filling. Of course, there's a whole range of different Irish recipes but traditional dishes are in general unfussy and usually based on easily available ingredients.

The Irish climate has a big influence on what crops are grown and what kind of foods are produced locally. All the rain that falls means plenty of excellent pasture for cattle. Beef, pork and lamb are very popular meats, while 'rashers' (strips of bacon), sausages and black and white pudding are part of the 'fry' or fried breakfast. The mountainous regions of the north and west of Ireland provide grazing for sheep sporting pink or blue splodges on their fleeces to identify them to their owners. Dairying is very strong in the rich pasturelands of the Golden Vale and the Galtee mountains in Munster. Milk, cream, cheese, butter and yogurt are also a big part of the Irish diet. Root vegetables like potatoes, carrots, sugar beet, cabbage and cauliflower are also produced locally so it's pretty well impossible not to eat your greens!

Fruity flavours

You'd never guess it but Sheep's Snout, Honey Ball and Irish Peach are just some of the names given to native varieties of apples! There were once about 140 different varieties of Irish apple. Armagh in Northern Ireland is known as the Orchard County because of its apple-growing tradition but apples, pears and plums are grown throughout Ireland. Rhubarb, berries and soft fruits like strawberries are also traditionally used in Irish baking. Every July, about 20,000 delicious tonnes of strawberries are sold at the County Wexford Strawberry Festival in Enniscorthy. This is the sunniest part of the island and so it's ideal for strawberry growing.

Fish for Friday

With ports dotted right around the coast, the fishing industry is very important and among the biggest ports are Killybegs, Dunmore East, Howth, Rossaveal and Castletownbere. Large quantities of fish are exported. Many people used to eat fish on Friday in particular. For religious reasons, meat would not be eaten on that day. Now you'll find festivals in Galway and Bantry where oysters and mussels are the stars. Although vegetarians have a wider choice than ever before, there is still a strong emphasis on meat on the average Irish menu.

Demand for prize-winning Irish farmhouse cheeses is strong both at home and abroad and a lot of these cheeses are vegetarian-friendly. Many of the small family-run cheese-making businesses are based in the rugged coastal mountains of West Cork.

Milleens is a soft cheese made from cow's milk with a flavour once described as a mix of farmyard, wet rocks and heather! Try **Gubbeen**, **Durrus** and **Cashel Blue** too.

The humble spud

The 'Irish apple' was actually a variety of potato that became very popular in the second half of the 18th century. Potatoes have always been central to the Irish diet and, in the past, were often the sole source of food for poor people (which explains why the famine of the mid-19th century was such a major catastrophe). Traditional Irish food will usually feature potatoes in some shape or form.

☞ **Champ** (or Pandy, Poundies, Cally) is based on mashed potatoes, creamy milk, a green vegetable like scallions (spring onions), chives, parsley or spinach and lots of melted butter. Champ was traditionally eaten with a spoon and would also have been served on Fridays, as a full meal rather than a side dish.

☞ **Boxty** is a potato bread which originated in Fermanagh, Cavan, Donegal and Leitrim. It's made from a mixture of mashed potatoes, grated raw potatoes, milk, flour and baking soda. If the mix is thinned with eggs and milk, you get pancakes.

The starchy water left over from boiling the potatoes would at one time have been used to stiffen shirt collars! The potato dough is shaped into scones called 'hurleys' which are boiled and then fried in a pan. The dough can also be cut into quarters called 'farls' and just baked. Farls are served as part of the Ulster fry and boxty pancakes can be filled with all sorts of savoury goodies.

Home baking

Traditionally, bread was made at home and every woman had her own version of the recipes! Yeast was less commonly used than bicarbonate of soda as a raising agent and so Irish breads are usually described as 'soda breads'. The most widely eaten variety is **brown bread**. It is made with a mix of wholemeal and plain white flour, buttermilk, and baking soda. The mixture is kneaded into a cake, crossed at the top using a knife (supposedly to let the fairies out!) and baked. White flour only is used to make **soda bread**. Adding sultanas, currants or raisins as well as sugar to the mix produces a delicious fruit bread. In Britain, **Spotted Dog** or **Spotted Dick** are a type of suet pudding but in Ireland, they are names for this fruit soda bread. It's also called **currany cake** (curranty cake) and **railway cake**.

Barm brack or **Hallowe'en brack** is a fruit bread usually shaped like a cake. It is made using yeast, which some say is where the 'barm' comes from, since barm is an old word for yeast. The other distinctive ingredient is cold tea which gives the bread its dark colour. Children watch each

other like hawks to see who gets the little ring hidden inside the brack. People used to say that the person who got the ring would marry within a year. Bracks used to contain other strange objects which foretold a person's future. A tiny piece of cloth meant poverty, a pea or a coin promised wealth, a piece of match warned that you could turn into a thug!

Weird and wonderful

Most children would run a mile from dried seaweed, but it is full of iron and minerals. In the west and northwest, it is sold as *dillisk* and as *carrageen moss*. Dillisk has the highest iron content of any edible food. It is a speciality of the annual Lammas fair in Ballycastle, Co. Antrim where it is known as *dulse*. Carrageen was commonly used to make milk puddings and was often given to patients to build up their strength.

☞ **Red lemonade** is so called because it's different from 'white' lemonade, which is in fact colourless! It is a popular mineral (a word you'll find to describe soft or fizzy drinks) in Ireland.

☞ Kimberley®, Mikado® and Coconut Creams® are biscuits which are gingery, marshmallowy, jammy and coconutty and made by the same company that invented the cream cracker.

☞ **Drisheen** is a speciality sausage from Cork made from a mixture of beef, milk and sheep's blood. It comes from an Irish word meaning 'intestine'. The usual name for blood pudding is black pudding, which is served along with white pudding in the Irish fried breakfast.

☞ **Irish stew** (a lamb stew with carrots, onions, potatoes and pearl barley) is famous but a less well-known Dublin stew is called **coddle**. Coddle is made with sausages and streaky bacon which are cut up and cooked between layers of potatoes and onions.

☞ Gourmets will appreciate a **Dublin Lawyer** without the silly wig. This is a lobster dish where the meat is sautéed in foaming butter. Whiskey is added to the pan and the whole lot is set alight. Finally, a generous helping of cream is added to the sauce and the meat is served in the lobster shells.

☞ **Crubeens** are pig's trotters that are simmered in a herby stock until the meat falls off the bone. They are

considered quite a delicacy which you eat with your fingers. In fact, every last bit of the pig used to be eaten. Even the bladder was inflated and used as a football in Ireland and wherever else ballgames were played. In American football, the ball is still referred to as a pigskin.

☞ **Grunt soup** has strictly nothing to do with pigs. It's a fish soup from Tyrone called after the perch or 'grunts' which are the main ingredient.

Two Dublin institutions

For 164 years, **Bewley's Oriental Cafés** were 'cathedrals of coffee-drinking' for all sorts of people, from writers James Joyce and Patrick Kavanagh to actor Cyril Cusack (father of four actresses well known to TV and theatre audiences in Ireland and abroad). The Irishwomen's Liberation Movement was founded in one of the cafés. The interiors had high ceilings, smoky wallpaper with oriental patterns, wooden chairs and heavy, marble-topped tables. The cafés were founded by the Bewley family, who came to Ireland in 1700. During the Second World War (known as the 'Emergency' in Ireland which remained neutral throughout), they were known for providing food for poor inner-city children. However, Celtic Tigers can't live on chat, coffee and sticky buns alone and in November 2004 the cafés were closed down. It was a sad day for many Dubliners.

Near Christchurch Cathedral, **Burdocks** is a well-known Dublin 'chipper' (chip shop) reputedly selling the best fish and chips in the city. The portions are 'ewidge' (Dublinese for 'huge') and very good value.

Festivals and National Celebrations

St Patrick's Festival (10–17 March, Dublin City)

St Patrick's Day is a big event in New York, Sydney, London, Munich and even Seoul in South Korea. Celebrations in Ireland used to be a bit quieter than those abroad. St Patrick's Day itself, 17 March, is a national holiday in Ireland. Colourful floats, marching bands and American majorettes parade through the main cities. People sport sprigs of shamrock in their buttonholes and small children wear badges with a ribbon in the green, white and orange colours of the Irish flag or with a golden harp emblem.

In 1996 the Irish government established the St Patrick's Festival to turn the one-day event into a national festival. A five-day street party was created and it now attracts more than a million visitors each year. The festival celebrates all things Irish, and combines the best of modern and traditional entertainment. There is non-stop street entertainment. Then there is the Skyfest, a huge computerized display of pyrotechnics, set to a soundtrack and involving more than 4,000 separate cues to set off fireworks. The final event, the Céilí Mór, is the biggest dance event in the country, guaranteed to get the city hopping.

Punchestown Races (late April, County Kildare)

Two weeks after Easter, the Irish National Hunt Festival, sometimes known as the Irish Cheltenham, takes place in Kildare. The Punchestown Races are such a major event in the area that schools and banks close for two days. But local schoolchildren go back to school two days earlier than everyone else at the end of the summer in order to make up for lost time!

The racecourse started off as a series of dry stone walls and natural banks, which formed perfect obstacles for the horses to clear. Racegoers could follow the race on foot. It was only in 1960 that artificial fences were constructed and the course began to be modernized. The first steeplechase prize of £300 has today grown to a Gold Cup worth €180,000.

Twelfth of July (Northern Ireland)

A sense of history is never far from the surface wherever you go in Ireland. In Northern Ireland, the month of July is often called the 'marching season' because of the number of parades that are held throughout the province. The high point for many people from the Ulster Unionist tradition in the North is 12 July, when as many as 3,000 parades take place. The sound of hundreds of fife-and-drum bands, including the booming 30-foot Lambeg drums, fills the air as thousands of people walk traditional routes to commemorate the Battle of the Boyne in 1690, a key moment in their ancestors' history. Banners displaying images of William of Orange astride a white horse are proudly carried by the marchers. Many of them wear bowler hats and orange sashes. The tradition of 'walking the Twelfth' is passed on from one generation to the next. A lot of marching bands travel around the province to take part in several parades.

Bloomsday (16 June, Dublin City)

On 16 June 1904 Leopold Bloom, the hero of James Joyce's novel *Ulysses*, goes on a 'voyage' around the city of Dublin. Every year on the same date, fans of the writer and his novel celebrate Bloomsday in the city. There are readings and re-enactments of scenes from the book. Many people dress up in Edwardian costume to recapture the flavour of early 20th-century Dublin in music and song. The fans with tough stomachs even sample the Bloomsday breakfast of Guinness and fried kidneys! You can make your own epic tour by following the 14 bronze plaques inlaid in the city-centre pavements. They mark major points on the route taken by Bloom as he wandered through the city.

Galway Arts Festival (12–24 July, Galway City)

This is one of Ireland's biggest and most popular festivals. As well as music, literature and comedy, you can see street theatre, children's drama, and a huge parade through the narrow Galway streets with

hundreds of performers. The Macnas Parade, the centrepiece of the festival, is a spectacular pageant with amazing creatures and fabulous costumes dreamed up by the Macnas Theatre Company. This Galway company has created shows and pageants for big events at home and abroad. They created the 20-metre figure of Gulliver that floated on the River Liffey in Dublin's Millennium celebrations in 1988. They also accompanied U2 on their huge Zooropa tour in 1993.

Puck Fair (10–12 August, Killorglin, County Kerry)

One of the most unusual Irish festivals, Puck Fair takes place over three days in August. As you'd expect, Fair Day features a horse fair, but the real star of the show is in fact a male goat. Every year on the August Bank Holiday Monday a wild goat minding his own business on a Kerry mountainside is captured and paraded through the streets of the small town of Killorglin, cheered on by the crowds. This is the Gathering Day, when the goat is crowned with great ceremony and becomes King Puck. He's raised on a 20-foot high platform above the crowds and for the next three days he becomes monarch of all he surveys, while his grateful subjects get to party. As well as the fair, there are open-air concerts, fireworks displays, street entertainers, dancing and plenty of fun. The last day, the Scattering Day, is when King Puck is taken down from his throne and returned to the wild once more.

There are a number of stories about the origins of King Puck. Like so many festivals in the Irish countryside, Puck Fair may date back to pre-Christian celebrations of the harvest. The most popular story about the fair's origins tells how the invading army of Oliver Cromwell was on the rampage in the district and scattered a herd of grazing mountain goats. One of the herd, a male goat, headed

towards Killorglin, while the others fled higher into the mountains. When the goat arrived exhausted in the town, the inhabitants knew that trouble was afoot and were able to escape harm. In establishing the festival and crowning the goat, the townspeople commemorate this event.

Ould Lammas Fair (last Monday and Tuesday of August, Ballycastle, County Antrim)

The Ould Lammas Fair in Ballycastle dates back to the 17th century. The feast of Lammas actually falls on 1 August, a date that coincides with the ancient Celtic harvest festival of Lughnasa. Lammas fairs traditionally took place all around the island, but the Ballycastle Lammas fair is the most popular for visitors to Northern Ireland. It has taken place for nearly 400 years. The MacDonnell family obtained a charter for the fair in 1606, and it is thought by some that it started as a series of exchanges between clans in Scotland and their relatives in Antrim. As well as the horsetrading and livestock sales that are the main business of the fair, there are market stalls, street entertainers, dancing and live music to keep everyone happy. One of the fair's specialities is *dulse*, which is an edible, sun-dried seaweed. The other, which is far more popular with children, is called Yellow Man. It is a type of sticky honeycomb sweet, which is sold in small chunks and could keep your dentist busy if eaten in large quantities.

Laytown Strand Races (September, County Meath)

Horse-racing is a year-round activity in Ireland, but one of the most unusual race meetings can only happen when the tide is out. Irish beaches are also called strands. Laytown Strand is a three-mile long beach on the sandy east coast to the north of Dublin. The first race on the strand is said to have taken place in 1876, but the regular gathering of racing enthusiasts started in 1901 and the tradition has continued ever since. The grandstand is constructed from a series of steps built into the sand dunes and, by the time the first race is ready to begin, the tide has very conveniently gone out. The races are unique in Europe as the only officially approved grandstand races that take place on a beach.

Galway International Oyster Festival (September, Galway City)

This festival started in 1954, when a hotel manager decided to promote the local speciality of oysters. The stars of the show are of course the oysters from Galway Bay. Did you know that an individual adult oyster can produce up to a million larvae in a single brood? But only about 250 will make it to adult life. The oyster can also change sex at least once in a lifetime!

You might not really like the sight or taste of oysters, but watching the World Oyster Opening Championship could be fun. Each competitor must open 30 oysters and display them according to very strict rules. Any bits of shell, grit or blood (gross!) on the oyster means that you lose points. The first person to complete the job satisfactorily wins the Championship. The world record is 1.31 minutes and it's held by an Irishman.

Passions Old and New

A Day at the Races

With its limestone soil and rich pastureland, Ireland is perfect for breeding horses, especially for racing. All racehorses are 'thoroughbreds', which means that they are bred purely for the purpose of racing and that their origins can be traced back to just three Arabian stallions in the eighteenth century: the Byerley Turk, the Darley Arabian and the Godolphin Arabian. All three were bred with English mares to produce faster, stronger horses ideal for racing conditions.

Kildare, nicknamed the Thoroughbred County, hosts international race meetings at the Curragh and Punchestown racecourses. The Irish National Stud is also located here and you can find out exactly where thoroughbred horses come from – with highly entertaining details!

There are three different types of races: flat racing (on level ground), jump racing (over obstacles) and the steeplechase (over fences of different sizes). The Irish Grand National on Easter Monday at Fairyhouse near Dublin is a steeplechase. The name was coined in 1752 in Cork by two men who wanted to settle a bet to decide which of them had the faster horse. They organised a race across country using two church steeples as the starting and finishing points.

An Irish racehorse that achieved great

international fame was Arkle. He won every major steeplechase in Britain and Ireland, and won the Cheltenham Gold Cup in England three times. A more recent star was Istabraq, who between 1998 and 2001 was the best hurdle horse in both islands. He is owned by the millionaire J. P. McManus, who also just happens to own a very large share of Manchester United Football Club!

Katie Riddle, Flex-a-Bill, Double O Seven, Mr Polo Bear, Kilcannon Explosion, New York Skyline, Drunken Disorderly, Fox in Flight, I Spy: have you ever wondered where on earth racehorses get their names from? Some foals' names make sense if you know the names of their parents. You might not think it, but there are strict rules for naming thoroughbreds. More than 4,000 names that are already in use by famous or successful horses are out of bounds, so there can be no Istabraq the Second. Other rules: no abbreviations, no numbers (unless they're spelt out), no notorious people such as Caligula or Hitler, no rude names. Have you noticed all the jokey names and puns? That's one area where people can get creative, so anything (well, nearly anything!) is possible.

Tools of the trad trade

Ireland is unique in having a musical instrument as its symbol. The emblem is based on a 14th-century harp. It's known as the BrianBorú harp, although it can't really have belonged to the 11th-century Viking-slayer. It can be seen today in Dublin's Trinity College.

One type of instrument that requires a good squeeze is the *uilleann* pipes. You use your elbow (*uilleann* in Irish) to squeeze air through the pipes and your fingers to play the notes. While they are absolutely perfect for playing sad songs (they wail really well), they sound great when combined with the beat of the *bodhrán*. This is a small drum played with the hand or a beater. It's made of goatskin (or even, sometimes, kangaroo skin) stretched over a wooden ring. Depending on how tightly the skin is stretched and where the player beats the *bodhrán*, the sound can vary greatly.

Traditional Irish musicians have always got together to play sessions. Around the country you will find musicians playing in pubs, in the street or pretty well anywhere. A festival of traditional Irish music is known as a *fleadh*. You will also find these festivals in countries with large Irish communities. One of London's longest running festivals is the Fleadh at Finsbury Park, which has been going for 14 years. The Irish national Fleadh takes place in different venues around Ireland and attracts thousands of fans every year. One of the best known and longest-running bands playing traditional Irish music is The Chieftains.

But you'll also hear traditional influences in music by The Pogues, Sinéad O'Connor, Van Morrison and Thin Lizzy! At more than three feet in diameter and producing up to 125 decibels, Northern Ireland's huge Lambeg drum is said to be the loudest drum in the world. During a performance by one drumming band their Lambeg was heard more than six miles away! The Lambeg has been around since the 17th century – long before amplifiers – and was originally used to signal troop movements and tactics on the battlefield.

Girls and boyz

Music is often a family affair and the Corrs are among the most famous Irish musical families. Their parents were also musicians. The three Corr sisters, Andrea, Sharon and Caroline, together with their brother Jim, were spotted during the making of *The Commitments*, a film about a fictional band in which Andrea played the band manager's sister. The Corrs have sold more than 18 million albums worldwide and their music has topped the charts in Australia, the UK, France and Spain. Another musical family are the Brennans from the Donegal Gaeltacht, who are better known as Clannad. They have sold more than 10 million albums, and their music can be heard on the soundtracks for the films *The Last of the Mohicans* and *Robin of Sherwood*. They are Irish-speakers. One of the sisters, Eithne, has a successful solo career as Enya. She is a little unusual

because she has never performed live. Ireland has exported a few boy bands too. First there was Boyzone, with Ronan Keating, and then there was Westlife. They were originally called Westside, but the name had already been used by an American band so they had to think again. Westlife are now in *The Guinness Book of Records* as the only band ever to top the charts seven times in a row. They've sold more than 34 million records and had 12 UK number ones. Bands like The Thrills, The Frames, Ash and Snow Patrol also have lots of fans.

For U2 it all started in 1977, when their drummer, Larry Mullen, posted an ad on the noticeboard of his north Dublin comprehensive school. More than 20 years later Ireland's biggest rock band is still packing stadiums and selling millions of albums worldwide. Their lead singer, Bono, is now well-known as a campaigner against poverty and disease in Africa, along with another Dubliner, Bob Geldof. When Bono first visited the White House, he was introduced to former President Clinton as 'a guy in jeans and a T-shirt with just one name'. He acquired that name from the sign over a hearing-aid shop called Bonavox. As often happens in Dublin, his friends shortened it and added an 'o' at the end. His real name is Paul Hewson.

Fancy footwork

In 1994 a seven-minute interval act in The Eurovision Song Contest, which was organized by the Republic of Ireland that year, started a phenomenon called *Riverdance*.

Children in Irish communities all over the world have always learned jigs, reels and hornpipes. In Irish dancing it is the feet that matter most. The steps are very complex and fast, but the rest of the body doesn't move.

Dancers wear soft shoes (a bit like ballet pumps) for some dances, and shoes with hard soles that allow them to beat out a rhythm for dances such as the hornpipe. Boys sometimes wear kilts. Girls' costumes can be very beautiful, with Celtic designs embroidered on the dresses and capes. One of the strangest things is the dancing wig. Girls traditionally wore ringlets, which bounced with the dancer's movements. Curling hair can be a pain in the neck and wigs have become popular, although they can itch like mad!

Most important for any top-level dancer is their ability to perform intricate dance steps without missing a beat. In the very early days of solo dancing a dancer had to dance on top of a barrel or on a slippery table surface to show just how good they were.

A Night at the Movies

Always fans of a good story, Irish people love 'the pictures'. People in the Republic are the most frequent cinemagoers in the European Union. Statistics in 2002 showed that people in Northern Ireland liked fantasy films and thrillers best, while comedy films were the hot favourites down South.

The man who designed the statuettes that actors are awarded at the Oscars was Cedric Gibbons, born in Dublin.

The Irish landscape regularly appears on the big screen. Films such as Disney's *King Arthur* (2004) and an earlier version of the Arthur legend, *Excalibur* (1981), were shot on location in County Wicklow. Well over 100 films have been shot at Ardmore Studios, which has been in

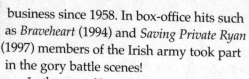

business since 1958. In box-office hits such as *Braveheart* (1994) and *Saving Private Ryan* (1997) members of the Irish army took part in the gory battle scenes!

In the past, films about Ireland itself gave a romantic Hollywood view of the country. The people were quirky and the actors, usually not Irish people, put on toe-curlingly awful Irish accents. The more recent films paint a very different picture. Some are gritty and funny. Others such as Jim Sheridan's *In America* (2003), the story of an Irish family living in New York, are gentle films.

The British director Alan Parker made *The Commitments* (1991), about a noisy bunch of Dubliners who form a band. The film was based on a book by a former teacher. (By the way, did you know that the actor Gabriel Byrne also used to teach kids? He once taught Spanish and drama in a Dublin school.)

Irish actors often have two careers, one in Hollywood and one at home. Colin Farrell started off in the popular BBC TV series *Ballykissangel* but these days he is one of Hollywood's big names. Both he and the Corkman Cillian Murphy starred in *Intermission* (2003), an Irish film that earned €2.7 million in just eight weeks, making it Ireland's biggest box-office hit ever.

The Irish government allows film companies to make films more cheaply, but they must produce up to 75 per cent of the film in Ireland itself. In exchange, people who want to invest money in making films pay less tax to the government. In the ten years since the tax deal was introduced, spending on film production has risen from £23 million to almost £100 million, and there has been a boom in Irish film-making, too. People are particularly keen on films about Irish topics. A surprise hit film in 1998, called *How to Cheat in the Leaving Certificate*, tells the story of six teenagers grappling with the dreaded final exams in June.

A Little Bit of Sport

Gaelic games

Gaelic football (also called just 'Gaelic'), hurling and camogie are very popular throughout the island. The games are unique to Ireland, but are played in countries with large Irish communities too. The first hurling match ever to be televised was actually played at Gaelic Park in New York in 1951. Each of the 26 counties in the Republic and the six counties of Northern Ireland has a junior and a senior team. Many of the county teams have nicknames. Kilkenny are the 'Cats', Dublin are the 'Dubs' and their rivals Kerry are known as 'the Kingdom'. The Galway team are the 'Tribesmen', Wexford are the 'Yellow Bellies' and Cork are the 'Rebels'. Teams from Ulster, Leinster, Munster and Connacht compete for a place in the All-Ireland finals at Dublin's Croke Park in September. Kilkenny, Cork and Tipperary are strong hurling counties, while Kerry has won the football championship 32 times, followed by Dublin with 22 wins. In 2002 Armagh made history by beating Kerry.

Gaelic was first played in the 17th century. Each team has 15 players. The game is fast. Players are allowed to shoulder-tackle each other and can use hands or fists to pass the ball to team-mates. The ball can also be held while running, but players must bounce it once – and once only – after every four steps, or drop it onto the foot, then kick it back into the hands. The goal area has both a net and a crossbar. Not surprisingly, when the ball goes in the net you score a goal!

If it goes over the crossbar, you gain a point. A goal is the equivalent of three points. The match lasts 70 minutes with a break after 35 minutes. About 3,500 schools around the country have Gaelic football teams. Girls' and ladies' football is also popular.

Hurling and camogie

Hurling is one of the fastest and most skilful field games in the world. It is so old that it even features in a number of ancient Irish legends. In the Middle Ages teams of up to 30 players would meet. By the late 19th century, county teams of 15 hurlers were playing each other according to set rules. The scoring system is similar to that used in Gaelic football. The hurley stick is made of ash wood and has a flat base to drive the ball, which is called a sliotar. The sliotar is made of leather, and is light and fast. Players now wear protective helmets, but this wasn't always the case. Children are coached in the game at school and team level.

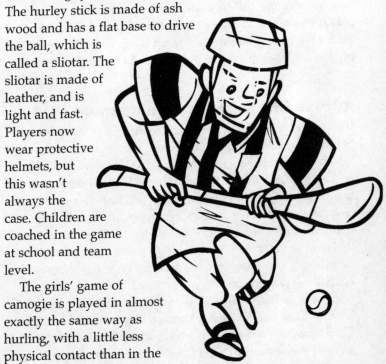

The girls' game of camogie is played in almost exactly the same way as hurling, with a little less physical contact than in the boys' game. Long ago girls used to play in long skirts, but they weren't allowed to use their skirts to block a ball!

International rules ok

This is a unique annual contest in which a Gaelic football team plays against an Australian Rules football team. The matches are played both in Ireland and in Australia. The series has been running since 1984, when Australia won the first contest in Dublin. The two types of football are similar in many ways. The Australian game was originally devised to keep cricketers fit during the winter season. It was first played in Melbourne in 1858. Although Australian footballers usually use an oval ball and play on an oval field, they use a round ball in the International Rules game and play on a standard rectangular pitch when in Ireland. The rules of the game are constantly updated. One of the best players of Australian footy was a Dubliner, Jim Stynes.

Across the water and back again

Irish soccer began mainly in Ulster, but by the 1880s it had become popular throughout Ireland. For historical reasons, separate football associations developed in Northern Ireland and in the Republic. Both still have their own international teams. The Republic's League of Ireland has a premier and a first division, and the 22 teams compete for the FAI Cup. The main venue for big matches is Lansdowne Road in Dublin.

There is a tradition, particularly among young Dubliners, of 'crossing the water' to play football in Britain. Many school-age players are spotted by British talent scouts or bought from Irish teams. Generations of players, from Johnny Giles to Roy Keane, Damien Duff and Kevin Kilbane, have made their mark on the beautiful game. When it comes to the European and World Cup tournaments, they go back

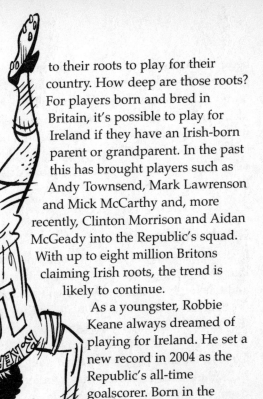

to their roots to play for their country. How deep are those roots? For players born and bred in Britain, it's possible to play for Ireland if they have an Irish-born parent or grandparent. In the past this has brought players such as Andy Townsend, Mark Lawrenson and Mick McCarthy and, more recently, Clinton Morrison and Aidan McGeady into the Republic's squad. With up to eight million Britons claiming Irish roots, the trend is likely to continue.

As a youngster, Robbie Keane always dreamed of playing for Ireland. He set a new record in 2004 as the Republic's all-time goalscorer. Born in the Dublin suburb of Tallaght, he began playing for his country at 17.

St Jack

The former England international Jack Charlton became the first non-Irish manager of the Republic of Ireland team in 1986. The team qualified for the European Championships in 1988 and 1992, and hit the World Cup trail in 1990, 1994 and 2002. Ireland's first-ever World Cup goal was scored by Kevin Sheedy in a match against England, a goal that had Irish fans dancing in sitting rooms, pubs and anywhere within an ass's roar of a telly. In the 1990s Jack Charlton became a national hero and was nicknamed 'St Jack'. He was given the freedom of the city of Dublin in 1994. Huge numbers of Ireland supporters travelled with the football teams and thousands more came out to welcome them home. The general public paid more attention than ever before to how Ireland was faring. Suddenly elderly ladies were checking the latest score with bus drivers listening to live coverage of the action.

Ruck and maul

Irish rugby is played at schools and universities. The Irish international team brings together players from the North and the South for the Triple Crown (playing England, Scotland and Wales), the Six Nations Cup (plus France and Italy) and the Rugby World Cup (everywhere else!).

Rugby was first brought to Ireland by students at Trinity College, Dublin. They had played the game at public school in England. The Irish game has a varied background, depending on where it is played. It was played in working-class Limerick in the early 20th century, while in Dublin it has been more popular with the wealthier middle class. It also has strong Ulster unionist roots. The big international fixtures are played at the Lansdowne Road stadium. Dublin's streets get lively as fans from Scotland, Wales, England and France descend on the city. Many wear kilts, daffodils or English roses. French fans once let loose an outraged cock on the rugby pitch! A recent major success for Ireland was the 2004 Triple Crown.

Going Places –
A Whistlestop
Tour of Ireland

Down the country

When you visit Ireland, you'll be looking at the road signs to guide you. In the South, you'll see signposts with the names in both English and Irish. In Northern Ireland, the signs are in English only. On both sides of the border, the place names often share the same history. The English names for most of them are a kind of echo of the original Irish sounds. When Ireland was a colony, the English authorities drew up military maps of the landscape, and renamed all the towns and villages using English spelling.

The place names can be quite long: try Ballynashannagh, or the brilliant Stranagalwilly. They can look like real tongue twisters. Why are they so long? Well, there are three or even four separate Irish words hidden just under the surface, but in English they are all run together to make up one megaword.

Not all names are long, though. There are even quite a few places called Inch (from the Irish for 'island')!

It can sometimes help to know what the Irish words actually mean. See if you can spot at least some of these words built into the place names when you're on your travels. They come from Irish words that describe some building or natural feature in the landscape.

Some names are mysterious. There's got to be a good story behind them: *Donegal* (fort of the foreigners), *Glasnevin* (stream of the child), *Glennawoo* (valley of the ghosts), *Lisnadill* (fort of the blind man). Places such as *Skiddernagh* (place of puddles), *Loughgall* (cabbage lake), *Knockcroghery* (hill of the hangman) or *Falcarragh* (scabby fence) might put you off if you took the names too literally. After all, *Rathgar* (rough fort) is one of the posher suburbs of Dublin! On the other hand, *Ardavagga* (height of merriment), *Clonmel* (pastures of honey) and *Tramore* (big strand) sound like the places to be. *Tonlegee* (backside to the wind), *Mausrower* (fat thigh) and *Ballyhack* (dwelling place of excrement) really make you wonder!

Dublin

The Celts named it after a river crossing and it's still called *Baile Átha Cliath* in Irish. Nearby was a place called Dubh

Linn ('black pool'). Around the year 837 along came the Vikings. They renamed it Dyflin. You can now wait for a bus while sitting in a replica longship at a spot marking the original Viking settlement.

Today about a third of the Republic's total population lives in the Greater Dublin area. The city has spread into the surrounding counties, where houses are less expensive. In the city itself, more and more people are now living in apartments.

The River Liffey divides the city into the 'Northside' and the 'Southside'. A rivalry between the two parts of the city has given rise to the claim that Northsiders 'eat their young' (meaning that they are not very civilized), while Southsiders are more refined. What a load of rubbish!

There are 14 bridges crossing the Liffey, including the Ha'penny Bridge, the metal bridge that people used to pay a toll of one (old) halfpenny to cross. The newest crossing, the James Joyce Bridge, was opened in 2003.

Belfast

Northern Ireland's capital is built on the River Lagan on the northeast coast. The first Norman castle there was built in the 12th century. In the 17th century the northeast of Ireland, including Belfast, was settled mainly by Scottish Presbyterians. French Huguenots also came to the city, bringing skills in weaving and textiles. The linen industry in Ireland began here and is still very important. A distinct culture developed. Belfast was the only city in Ireland to become industrialized in the 19th century. Many of the city's buildings date from the Victorian period.

In 1898 the author of *The Chronicles of Narnia*, C.S. Lewis, was born in Belfast.

The world's biggest ship, the *Titanic*, was built and launched at Belfast's Harland & Wolff shipyard in 1911. It was 269 metres (883 feet) long. The modern shipyard also built Dublin's James Joyce Bridge.

In 1941, during the Second World War, 900 people were killed in Belfast during a single air raid by German bombers, more than any other city apart from London. Fire engines were sent from as far away as Dublin to try to put out the fires.

111

Things to do or see in and around Belfast:

☞ Visit the Ulster Museum and see treasures from the *Girona*, one of the 20 ships from the Spanish Armada that sank off the northern and western coasts of Ireland in 1588.

☞ Find out how the world works by using the interactive science exhibits at Belfast's whowhatwherewhenwhy – W5. The exhibition's five main areas are called Wow, Start, Go, See and Do.

☞ See Belfast City Hall, built when Queen Victoria gave Belfast city status in 1888.

☞ Take a black taxi tour around the city, and see the murals on the Falls and Shankill Roads.

☞ See Samson and Goliath, the giant cranes in Belfast's dockland. Built in the early 1970s, they are both more than 300 feet high. They can carry loads of up to 840 tonnes.

For 35 years Belfast has been in the headlines around the world because of the conflict between the different communities living there. Districts in the city are still very clearly identified as Catholic or Protestant. In 1998 the Belfast Agreement began the process of working towards a peaceful future for the city and for Northern Ireland as a whole.

Cork

Situated on the south coast, on the River Lee, the Republic's second city is an important port. The city's Latin motto means 'a safe harbour for ships'. It started out as a monastic settlement founded by St Finbarr around the year 606, and was developed by the Vikings. It received its charter as a city in 1185, from Prince John.

Belfast Opera House

In 1491 a man named Perkin Warbeck arrived in the city and claimed to be the rightful heir to the English throne. The great pretender had the support of many of the kings of Europe, as well as the city of Cork, but failed in his attempt. He was executed along with his followers (including the Lord Mayor of Cork, John Water) at Tyburn in 1499.

In the 18th century, Cork was the world's largest butter market and its butter was salted especially for export.

During the period of the war of independence from Britain and in the Irish civil war that followed, both the city of Cork and the county named after it were deeply involved in the fighting. Michael Collins, whose story features in a

---

Things to do or see in and around Cork:

☞ Climb up the red and white steeple of St Ann's church and ring the bells of Shandon.

☞ Visit the Butter Museum and then sample Cork's salty butter.

☞ Visit the wildlife park on Fota Island.

☞ Kiss the Blarney Stone and never shut up again!

Shandon Steeple

film by Neil Jordan, started and finished his life in County Cork. The city lost two more Lord Mayors during this period: one was murdered and the other died on hunger strike in Brixton Prison.

Cork is a university city with a lively film, theatre and arts scene. It is currently undergoing major development and is the European Capital of Culture for 2005.

Galway

Galway began as a small fishing village at the mouth of the River Corrib on the west coast. The name is thought to mean 'place of foreigners'. By 1235, the first Normans had arrived to claim the surrounding lands. The original inhabitants were not amused and one family has gone down in local history as 'the ferocious O'Flahertys'. Fourteen other merchant families of Norman English descent followed. Their family surnames were Athy, Blake, Bodkin, Browne, D'Arcy, Deane, Ffont, Ffrench, Joyce, Kirwan, Lynch, Martin, Morris and Skerritt. In time, Galway became known as the 'City of the Tribes' thanks to these families. The merchants developed the town into a prosperous port. Trade with continental Europe and the West Indies flourished. Galway's fortunes declined after it was taken by Cromwell's armies in 1652.

Things have changed since then. Galway is now one of the fastest-growing cities in Europe and has recently become the Republic's

third-largest city. It is a lively university city, with the sea and the mountains of Connemara within easy reach. There are festivals of every kind in this city, and the Galway races too.

There is a very popular ring that, in Ireland, is associated with Galway. The Claddagh was once an old fishing village, now part of Galway City, and the Claddagh ring takes its name from there. It is worn by men and women as a token of love. The design shows two hands holding a heart, which

---

Things to do or see in and around Galway:

☞ Visit the Spanish Arch, the remains of a 16th-century bastion built onto the city walls to protect Galway's merchant ships, including Spanish galleons, from looters. The City Museum is also here.

☞ Take a boat or plane to the Aran Islands, right on the edge of Europe. You can see spectacular traces of Ireland's Celtic past here. The biggest of the three islands is Inis Mór. It is about 14 kms (8.7 miles) in length and 3.8 kms (2.4 miles) in width. Hundreds of dry stone walls carve up the tiny fields, which the islanders had to create, using sand, seaweed and imported soil. This is where the white woollen Aran sweaters come from.

☞ At Kylemore Abbey, see what it's like to go to school in an 18th-century castle.

bears a crown. If the ring is worn with the heart pointing inwards towards the knuckle, it means that the wearer loves someone and their heart is 'taken'. A ring worn with the heart pointing outwards towards the finger nail means that the wearer's heart is still free.

Limerick

The city was founded by the Vikings at the mouth of the River Shannon. It got its charter as a city in 1197, and the huge King John's Castle was built between 1200 and 1212. The castle made Limerick a garrison city and it became the centre of English power in the west.

Limerick was besieged three times during the 17th century. The most famous siege took place a month after the Battle of the Boyne in 1690, when the armies of the defeated James II retreated to Limerick. William of Orange's armies followed and

Kylemore Abbey

Treaty Stone

bombarded the city, but did not succeed in taking it until the following year. The townswomen of Limerick were particularly fierce in defending the city. A second siege ended when a deal was struck promising lands and greater religious freedom in exchange for the city's surrender. The deal, called a treaty, was broken, however, and harsh laws were put in place instead.

Rugby has a long tradition in Limerick, and is played by dockers and doctors alike. Every autumn, rugby teams from Australia and New Zealand come to play against the Munster team. After Munster beat New Zealand's All Blacks

---

Things to do or see in and around Limerick:

☞ Visit King John's Castle and climb the battlements.

☞ Find out more about the sieges at the castle.

☞ See the Treaty Stone, which commemorates the end of the siege of 1691.

☞ See the cross worn by Mary Queen of Scots on the day of her execution, on display at the Hunt Museum.

☞ Visit one of Ireland's most important pre-Celtic sites at Lough Gur. It dates back to 3000 BC. You can see the remains of a crannóg or lake dwelling from the lake shore.

☞ Visit Bunratty Castle and Folk Park in Country Clare.

team in 1978 the winning players were treated like heroes.

There once were two cats from Kilkenny
Each thought there was one cat too many
So they fought and they fit
And they scratched and they bit,
Till instead of two cats there weren't any.

No one knows what the exact link is between the city and the funny five-line verse called a limerick, which the poet and artist Edward Lear made popular in the 19th century. Short, funny poems written by 18th-century Irish poets living near the city are said to be very similar in style. They often made fun of people in public life.

Guildhall, Derry

Derry

Northern Ireland's second city lies on the River Foyle, near the border with County Donegal, which is in the Republic. The Irish name for Derry means 'oak grove' and the original site may have been sacred for the druids. In the sixth century St

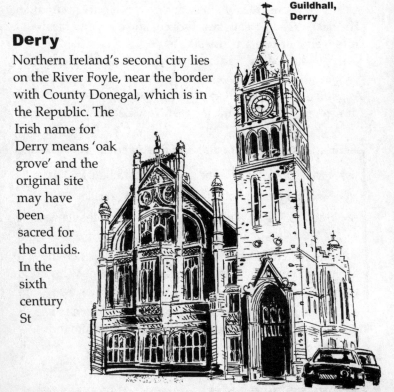

Columcille founded a monastery here.

In 1613, during the plantation of Ulster, Derry's link with a number of wealthy London companies was established and the plantation city became known as Londonderry. The city's walls date from this time and it remains the only completely walled city in Ireland (there are none in Britain).

Like Limerick, Derry also underwent a major siege in 1689. This time it was William's Protestant supporters inside the city who held off James II's forces. The city's gates had been closed in 1688 by 13 apprentices and stayed shut for 105 days. The citizens inside the walls were forced to eat rats and dogs, and about 7,000 of the city's 30,000 people died of starvation and disease. The siege was eventually broken. Every year, on 12 August, a parade commemorates the event.

You can still hear two names for the city: Derry/Londonderry or Londonderry/Derry. A radio DJ jokingly called it 'Stroke City', rather than pick one of the two names. This is the city that produced punk pop group The Undertones in 1975. They were catapulted to fame when DJ John Peel played 'Teenage Kicks' on BBC Radio in 1978.

Every year you can see up to 40,000 people running around in costumes during the city's five-day Hallowe'en Carnival on the banks of the Foyle. It's the largest Hallowe'en celebration on the island.

A Way With Words

I rish people speak English with a range of different accents. The Belfast accent is distinctly different from the Dublin or Cork accent. Sometimes people speak very quickly. The following list gives just a few words and expressions you might hear, plus some examples to show how they are used. (D) means that it is a mostly a Dublin word; (N) means that it's usually heard in Northern Ireland.

Guess what the following expressions mean:

☞ *He'd mind mice at a crossroads.*

☞ *Have a titter of wit!*

☞ *It's the quiet pig that eats the meal.*

Do you give up?

☞ He's very capable, and even a bit cunning.

☞ Have some common sense!

☞ Some people talk alot. Others just get things done.

Everyday things

boreen	small country road	
citeog	left-handed person (say kit**ogue**)	
delph	crockery, dishes	
gansey	jumper, sweater	
hot press	airing cupboard	
messages	shopping	*I'm going to get the messages.*
press	cupboard	
scallions	spring onions	
to wet the tea	to make the tea	*Did you wet the tea?*
yoke	thing, thingummy	*What's that yoke for?*

Positive noises

after doing	just done	*He's after phoning for a taxi.*
amn't I?	aren't I?	*I'm coming too, amn't I?*
to go asleep	to go to sleep	*I couldn't go asleep I was so excited.*
crack / craic	fun	*It's good crack. We did it for the crack. She's great crack.*
a dote	a sweet person, especially a child	*He's a little dote.*
fair play (to you)!	well done!	
a fine thing	a handsome boy or man	*Colin Farrell is a fine thing.*
game ball! (D)	excellent! you're on!	
a gas ticket	funny person	*She's a gas ticket.*
grand	great, fine	*That's grand. I'm grand, thanks. That'll do grand.*
a wain (N)	a child	
will	shall (in Ireland, people use *will* rather than *shall*)	
	Shall we go for a walk?	*Will we go for a walk?*
	What shall we do now?	*What will we do now?*

Negative vibes

banjaxed (D)	broken, useless	*The TV's banjaxed, we'll have to get a new one.*
a blow-in	an outsider	*a crowd of blow-ins from Dublin.*
bockety	rickety, unsteady	*a bockety chair.*
bold	naughty	*Don't be so bold.*
to cod	to joke	*I'm not codding you.*
cute	cunning	*as cute as a fox.*
an eejit	a twit, an idiot	*a right eejit. You big eejit!*
to foother	to fiddle, fuss about	*Stop foothering around and lay the table.*
to give out	to complain, moan	*That one never stops giving out.*
to give out to	to tell off	*The teacher gave out to him for forgetting his homework.*
		My dad gave out stink to me.

123

a grind	a private lesson (extra tuition)	*She's getting grinds in Irish.*
a head-the-ball (D)	an individual who is pretty well bonkers	
a land	a let-down	*We got a land when we found the cinema was shut.*
a mill	a fight, a scrap	*a big mill in the playground.*
a scut	a rascal	
wrecks my head	does my head in	*That teacher just wrecks my head.*
your man	a male you are talking about	*See your man over there, he went to school with my dad.*
your woman	a female you are talking about	*Who does your woman think she is?*

Some other expressions

to act the maggot	to mess about
to go for a dander (N)	to go for a stroll
to be on the pig's back	to be doing well, to be successful
to throw the head	to throw a wobbler, to lose it
to throw shapes (D)	to act cool
to be a bit of a bungalow	to have nothing on top (i.e. be a bit thick)
to make a hames of	to mess up completely
you have your glue! (D, older)	you've got a nerve!
not to put a tooth in it	to be very blunt, not to mince words

Return of the unpronounceables?

Not at all – have a go! You put the emphasis on the sounds in bold typeface when saying these Irish words, which have all cropped up earlier in this book.

An Lár	un **lawr**	the city centre
bodhrán	bauw**rawn**	small hand-held Irish drum
céilí	**kay**lee	a get-together for dancing
Cúchulainn	Koo**kull**in	a mythical hero
currach	**curr**ock	fishing boat

Dáil	**dawl**	the Irish House of Commons
Éire	**Aira**	Ireland
Éireann	**Airenn**	of Ireland (used in lots of official names)
Fáilte	**fawl**tcha	Welcome
fleadh	**flah**	traditional music festival
Gaeilge	**gwayl**guh	the Irish language
gaelscoileanna	**gwayle**skullena	Irish-speaking schools
Gaeltacht	**gwale**tokt	an Irish-speaking area
Garda	**gaw**rda	a police officer
Oireachtas	ir**oktus**	the Irish parliament
piseóg	pis**hogue**	a superstitious custom
seanchaí	shana**kee**	a storyteller
Slán	**slawn**	Goodbye
Sláinte	**sloyn**tcha	Cheers, Good health
Taoiseach	**tee**shock	Irish Prime Minister
uilleann	**illen**	elbow (for Irish bagpipes)

When writing people's names, you'll find that the little dash (called a *fada*) on the vowels matters to many people, but you'll also find the names written without it.

Girls' names	**sounds like**	**Boys' names**	**sounds like**
Dearbhla	**derv**la	Ciarán	kier**awn**
Eithne	**eth**na	Diarmuid	**deer**mid
Niamh	**neeve**	Niall	nile/neil
Róisín	**roh**sheen	Oisín	**us**heen
Siobhán	shiv**aun**	Pádraic	**paw**(d)rik

Irish into English

Did you know that some common English words have come from Irish Gaelic?

galore	(as in toys and presents galore)
slogan	(an advertising slogan like 'Just do it!')
smithereens	(smashed to smithereens)
Tory	(conservative, as in the Tory Party)
to twig	(to understand. *Suddenly I twigged.*)

Good Books

Fiction books

Conlon-McKenna, Marita, *The Children of the Famine Trilogy: Under the Hawthorn Tree, Wildflower Girl* and *Fields of Home*, O'Brien Press

Conlon-McKenna, Marita, *Safe Harbour,* O'Brien Press

Lenihan, Eddie, *Gruesome Irish Tales for Children* and *Rowdy Irish Tales for Children,* Mercier Press

Lingard, Joan, *The Kevin and Sadie Quintet: The Twelfth Day of July, Across the Barricades, Into Exile, A Proper Place* and *Hostages to Fortune,* Penguin Books (Puffin Modern Classics)

Loughrey, Eithne, *The Annie Moore Trilogy: First in Line for America, The Golden Dollar Girl* and *New York City Girl,* Mercier Press

Macken, Walter, *Flight of the Doves,* Pan Books

Macken, Walter, *The Irish Trilogy: Seek the Fair Land, The Silent People* and *The Scorching Wind,* Pan Books

Morpurgo, Michael, *The Ghost of Grania O'Malley,* Egmont

Scott, Michael, *Irish Myths and Legends,* Time Warner Books

Non-fiction books

Flanagan, Deirdre and Laurence, *Irish Place Names,* Gill & Macmillan

Galvin, Tom, *The Little Book of Dublin,* New Island Press

Llewellyn, Morgan, *Granuaile, the Pirate Queen* and *Brian Boru, Emperor of the Irish,* O'Brien Press